PERSEVER

HOW HIBERNIAN SMASHE

BIGGEST CURSE IN FOOT

PERSEVERED

HOW HIBERNIAN SMASHED THE
BIGGEST CURSE IN FOOTBALL

AIDAN SMITH

First published in Great Britain in 2016 by
ARENA SPORT
An imprint of Birlinn Limited
West Newington House
10 Newington Road
Edinburgh
EH9 1QS

www.arenasportbooks.co.uk

ISBN: 9781909715479
eBook ISBN: 9780857909213

British Library Cataloguing-in-Publication Data
A catalogue record for this book is available on request from the
British Library.

Designed and typeset by Polaris Publishing, Edinburgh
www.polarispublishing.com

Printed in Great Britain by TJ International Ltd, Padstow, Cornwall

CONTENTS

For Archie

INTRODUCTION

HIGH SUMMER IN the Lang Toon. A mother screams at her daughter dressed in a matching shellsuit outside a Cash Generator. A seagull swoops on a discarded fudge doughnut. Three boys with fishing rods point and laugh at the encumbered bird's struggles to regain altitude. I have returned to where it all began and Kirkcaldy is beautiful.

The oldest football competition in the world, featuring the most blighted, benighted, winless and wobegone, hapless and hoodoo-ed club on the planet. Hibernian's epic disinclination towards the Scottish Cup was a gripping, macabre tale, re-told every year, and always ending the same way: with defeat. Sometimes at Hampden, the national stadium, other times in tough little towns like this, where tough little teams lurk.

Shops are closed because they're on holiday although many are on permanent vacation. In the High Street there's a pawnbroker face-off and presumably these rival bawbees-for-cash outlets regularly knock three bells out of each other to offer the best deals. But if that suggests a place down on its luck, who was really going to flog the family jewels so they could place a bet on Hibs ending the curse after 114 years and lifting the trophy, especially when their entry into the 2015-16 competition was an away tie at Raith Rovers?

There's plenty of local colour here with which to compose an over-the-top epitaph for an underachieving football team. There's a bar called The Exchequer which, even if there's no connection with the former Chancellor and Rovers fan, prompts you to wonder: what would a Gordon Brown theme pub actually be like? There's a nightclub called Blue Monday and much as I hoped to find a 'Closed on Mondays' notice on the door I have to be truthful and say that in Kirkcaldy the

1980s retro beat seems pretty relentless. And there's a baker's shop that's been going since 1857, longer even than Hibs' cup affliction, its success based on products which haven't failed to rise, haven't gone all gooey in the middle when a tougher consistency was ordered, unlike the team from across the water in the port of Leith.

This will be no obituary.

1902 was when the cup was last returned to Hibs' home, Easter Road, but we don't need to hear of it again. No more Buffalo Bill, no more Edward VII, no more Charles R. Debevoise. These three can go back to being regular 1902 dudes and stop piggybacking on the club's failure.

One was a hero of the American Wild West and would turn up in accounts of Hibs' regular flopping simply because in 1902 he wasn't yet dead and namechecks usefully illustrated just how long the jinx had been in existence. Another was sat on the throne in 1902 while the third, who was similarly rescued from dusty history books to enjoy unexpected attention, invented the brassiere that year.

Two cups? Hibs just wanted one.

But I've come back to Kirkcaldy to walk up to Raith's stadium, Stark's Park, wondering if I'll return regularly now. Wondering indeed if there's a small-business opening for a heritage trail, a green plaque-dotted tour which would have to begin right here, close to the pentecostal church promoting 'Faith, hope, love'. The strolling lecture would tell how Hibs ended the cycle of despair and stopped being the biggest joke in Scottish football, the most tragic case in the game globally. These weren't official titles but we were claiming them anyway. For long enough, they were just about all we had to our name.

This is how Hibs won the Scottish Cup. Yes, they actually did it: *Hibs won the Scottish Cup*. First, though, a keen academic debate . . .

ONE

v : HIBS IT

IT IS MARCH 2016 and in the offices of the *Oxford English Dictionary,* words and phrases fly around all day long. New words and perky phrases, all of them seeking acceptance. It is the job of the staff to sort the wheat from the chaff, to say nothing of the chavs, and distinguish between the neologisms which add to the gaiety of the nation and describe The Way We Live Now – and those chancer, too-trendy buzzwords which are mere fluff and will be quickly forgotten.

Hibsing it.

But it's a war of words in this place. There are in fact two offices: the original, more than a century old with staff not much younger, and the newish extension. One – dusty, fusty – looks like a place of work while the other seems to be a place of play. Parked between items of dayglo furniture are kiddies' trikes. These are clichés of groovy office-life but this room's bearded hipsters – another cliché – don't care about that. They ride the trikes, chasing each other, pursuing words.

The two divisions don't get on, there's a deep mistrust. They're separated by some high filing cabinets; the oldsters wish for a moat with huge vats of oil suspended above, nicely boiling. The oldsters think the youngsters too impetuous; the young brigade think their elders too resistant to change. But there has to be change. According to the most recent survey, people are using fewer and fewer words.

They're trying to get through their daily lives with the bare minimum, an average of seventeen at the last count. The language is dying.

Hibsing it.

So the oldsters, who have the last word on new words, are bombarded with recommendations from their wacky colleagues. Some are scrawled on paper aeroplanes and fired at them. Others are sent by email, suddenly bursting onto the screens of the dictionary veterans and flashing in big capital letters to blaring pop music. Generally baffled by computers, the oldsters have to call the kids over to get the would-be words removed.

HIBSING IT!

The greyhairs are particularly unimpressed by applications for sports words, believing that football people have mangled quite enough of the lexicon already. Managers and players are reckoned to have been poorly-educated, a problem compounded by media-training which ensures they say nothing original or interesting. Post-match, the dry, stale air of low-ceilinged interview rooms is filled with hackneyed comments about taking each game as it comes, giving the other team respect and normally landing in row Z with that kind of shot, to be fair. A new football word would have to be remarkably clever, witty and vital to impress the grizzled and grumpy guardians of the *OED*.

The bid to have 'Hibsing it' ratified and verified comes from a Heart of Midlothian supporter. Hearts, the Jam Tarts, the Jambos, are the Edinburgh rivals of Hibernian, Hibs, the Hibees. Hearts fans enjoy seeing Hibs suffer, fail, be relegated, almost die, lose cup finals, lose to anyone, but there's a kind of losing which Jambos reckon Hibs do better and more consistently than anyone else – that is to lose from a highly advantageous position, when you really should be winning. To snatch defeat from the jaws of victory. To do a Devon Lock, after the horse cantering to glory only to perform the splits just before the finish-line. To do a Don Fox, in the style of the Rugby League Challenge Cup hero-apparent who sliced what should have been the winning kick. To be Wile E. Coyote, having snared the Roadrunner at last, only to be flattened by a plummeting boulder. To be Tom, cooking himself a Jerry-based dinner at last, only to be pancaked by a flying anvil. To be Tom Courtenay in *Billy Liar*, who wins gorgeous Julie Christie then lets her leave town on a train. This is Hibsing it.

The phrase gets the full backing of the young bucks at the next applications meeting and there's predictable harrumphing from the dictionary's senior division. You cannot really believe that in 2015 these guys passed sexting and twerking and shiny-bum the year before. The younger element press the case, tell the story of the club, how they were formed in 1875, won the Scottish Cup a couple of times around the turn of the century, won three league titles with a brilliant forward line called the Famous Five and were the first British club to compete in the European Cup, produced some fine sides after that, notably Turnbull's Tornadoes, and although they occasionally lifted the League Cup, the Hibee narrative is invariably one of flattering to deceive.

The grandads, as the kids call their long-serving colleagues, are made to watch a film of Hibs purporting to Hibs it, including a number of games against Hearts. There's the one where the Hibees captain taunted Jambos with '7-0' dyed into his hair in recognition of a famous derby drubbing only for his team to throw away a two-goal lead in stoppage time. There's the one where Hibs fans turned up with balloons and streamers to hold a 'relegation party' for their doomed foes, only to lose the game and end up being demoted along with them.

And there's the playoff which condemned them to that fate when, as the Scottish Premiership team, they'd won 2-0 at Hamilton Academical from the lower division and would surely secure their safety at home, only to be dragged down into the Championship after a penalty shootout. They're still there now.

Unimpressed, the carriage-clock contenders acknowledge Hibs are a biggish club who should have achieved more, and that, yes, the manner in which they'd contrived to blow some games was pretty spectacular, but don't all teams do this now and again? And anyway, how bad could Hibs really be if they'd managed to win the Scottish Cup a couple of times around the turn of the century?

No, not the turn of *this* century, the turn of the last one. Their previous victory was way, way back in 1902.

The oldsters are stunned. That's very nearly as ancient as the dictionary!

TWO

'YEE-HA!'

MAY, 2001, HIBS versus Celtic, won by the Glasgow team, three goals the margin. On paper this doesn't sound terribly dramatic. In the context of Hibs' Scottish Cup travails it sounds standard-issue. Celtic had previously lifted the cup by inflicting that level of defeat on the Hibees and would do so again later.

But the one in 2001 turned ninety-nine into a hundred. Turned up the pressure, turned up the joke count. A whole century of failure transformed 1902 into a stonker of a year.

Nestling in the history books between 1901 and 1903, 1902 had no idea it would become so desperate for Hibs fans and so beautiful to supporters of Hearts. It had to wait until Hibs failed to win the cup at the ninety-ninth time of asking but the team duly obliged. Sure, it was mentioned previously as Hibs tried and failed, more and more often as the wait got closer and closer to a hundred years. Then 1902 became properly sexy.

It became a specialist subject for Jambos keen to test their brainpower on Mastermind. 'You have two minutes to answer questions on 'Other Things That Happened in 1902 Besides the Frankly Hilarious Fact of it Being the Year Hibernian Last Won the Scottish Cup'. Your time starts ... now:

'Who was William Frederick Cody better known as?'

'Buffalo Bill.'

'What did he have to do to earn the nickname?'

'Win an eight-hour bison shoot.'

'What was the final result?'

'He shot sixty-eight bison to William Comstock's forty-eight.'

'In an eighteen-month period between 1867-68 what was the total number of bison brought down by Buffalo Bill?'

'4,282.'

'Name five other notable events which occurred in 1902.'

'Edward VII was crowned King of Great Britain. The brassiere was invented. The vacuum cleaner was invented. The Boer War ended. Real Madrid were formed.'

This was undoubtedly impressive. Maybe the Jambos consulted their leatherette-bound *Reader's Digest* to end up so knowledgeable although in any case 1902-centred info was churned out by TV and the newspapers in handy history fun-pack form every time Hibs resumed the quest for the cup, and especially after the defeat in 2001.

But when Hibs played Celtic that year, something happened which would eventually change the club's image, status, personality, DNA, everything. Only we didn't know it back then and neither did Celtic's half-time substitute.

This wasn't the cup final but the dress-rehearsal in the Scottish Premier League three weeks before. The game at Easter Road was televised live, with the odd kick-off time of 6.05pm on a Sunday evening. Because of this, and the fact the teams would soon be meeting at Hampden in a more glamorous context, the crowd was a modest 8,728.

There was fantastic talent on show. Henrik Larsson, Lubomir Moravcik, Franck Sauzee and Russell Latapy were among Scottish football's greatest-ever foreign stars, although something else we didn't know was that this would be the last occasion Latapy would pull on a too-big Hibs shirt and take the ball for an extensive meander.

The Hibs manager, Alex McLeish, bombed out the little Trinidadian playmaker after a drinking session ended with him in a car trundling the wrong direction down a one-way street. Could Latapy have won Hibs the cup? McLeish's team were attractive and yet strong, two qualities which for Hibs don't often mix. But their fine form had slipped from the first half of the season when they thumped Hearts 6-2 and split the Old Firm going into the winter break. The magic usually came from the patter-merchant Latapy, though, and the fans would debate whether the manager's disciplinarian rule, doubtless learned from playing under Alex Ferguson, served Hibs best or whether you should always make allowances for tearaway genius.

Hibs put up a decent show in the final. Close, as Buffalo Bill might have said, but no clay pipe. Larsson scored a late penalty to give his team a comfortable 3-0 victory.

Alan Stubbs was a substitute that day, as he had been in the league game, which marked his comeback after a six-month battle against cancer. When he took the field at Easter Road just after seven o'clock on a beautiful late spring evening he was greeted with warm applause – not just from the Celtic fans but the Hibs supporters too. The big Scouser was touched, even more so when he scored the fourth of Celtic's five goals and Hibbies chanted his name.

Stubbs never forgot that welcome; it confirmed Hibs as a good club with decent values. Obviously, a new manager doesn't choose his first post based purely on an emotional impulse. Stubbs will have given pragmatic consideration to all the options before deciding to take the job. But to have so many fans of a rival club rooting for him as he returned from the darkness undoubtedly played a part in his decision.

'To get a reception like that is something that will live with me to the very end,' Stubbs said in June 2014 on his first day as Hibs boss. 'This is a chance for me to repay it and hopefully the fans will give a reception to my team when they see the type of football they play. I want them to be proud of the team, that's the most important thing.'

In 2001 the only consolation that seemed available to Hibs for losing that final was in the living-history project they became for the nation so everyone could learn a little bit more about what life was like at the turn of the previous century. Journalists worked diligently to provide this detail. Instead of chasing up-to-the-minute news they competed with each other for the most fancy-that facts about 1902 to better emphasise the boggling amount of time elapsed since the trophy engraver last steadied his hand to make the telling gouge 'Hibernian'.

When editors were satisfied that all of Scotland knew that Buffalo Bill was still alive and well in 1902 they reckoned the masses were keen for more info on the celebrity bison-basher so they put their most dogged, married-to-the-job, sleep-in-their-cheap-suits investigative reporters on the case. The newshounds discovered that around the same time Bill was a touring Wild West roadshow superstar shooting up Scotland with his yee-ha spectacular. This was a stunning revelation, and more incidental detail with which to embroider the sorrowful Hibee saga of the ever-elusive cup. Bill left a trail of mayhem including burned-down Dundee goods yards and deserted Aberdeenshire trawlers – the price of fish rocketed because the crews were all at his show. He climbed Edinburgh's Calton Hill, declaring 'Ain't she a beaut!', and even attended a Rangers-Queen's Park match.

Hearts fans loved this. 'Let's all laugh at Hibees,' they taunted. Mock photos of the 1902 victory parade appeared, showing the most antiquated of horse-drawn transport options, in truth not much older than the vehicle used in the procession. Hibbies could do little but add to the mirth. 'When the Hibs go up to lift the Scottish Cup,' they sang in 2001, 'we'll be dead.'

But as the sun set on Russell Latapy's career, it was ever so slightly starting to rise on that of a future Hibs hero. There was sunshine on Leith when Alan Stubbs ran onto the pitch in that league game, a few years before the song was ever heard at games.

THREE

'I WANT TO TAKE ALL THE CANCER FROM ALAN . . .'

AN OLD LECTURER at journalism college, when he was explaining the art of writing a newspaper story and how you had to hook the readers with a smart intro, liked to replay his greatest hits from long years in the ink trade. 'Women look much smaller with their clothes off,' he once declared apropos of nothing, 'but footballers look much smaller with theirs on.'

You couldn't get away with that sort of thing now. But was it even true? Alan Stubbs, fully clothed, has just appeared in the doorway of the cafe and he's filling it like the bad guy in a comic-strip and blocking out the sun. He's immense.

The point I guess my tutor was trying to make about footballers is that when you meet them away from the pitch out of their kit they shrink. Footballers can certainly look huge when you're a small boy peering over the terrace wall at them thrashing your team. In 1968, when I was deemed old enough for a match featuring the Old Firm, Celtic came to Easter Road and said to Hibs: 'Go on, dare to take the lead. With only eleven minutes left, see if we don't roar back with four great goals.'

Celtic were terrifying just running onto the park. Three regular Gigantors led the way: Billy McNeill, Bobby Murdoch, John Hughes. Maybe it was those hoops stretched across barrel chests which made them seem so much bigger than the Hibs players. Even wee Jimmy

Johnstone – who I thought was no taller than the boys kicking empty fag packets in pub doorways while their fathers downed pints of heavy inside – cast a long cartoon shadow that day. The final score was Hibs 2, Celtic 5, just as it had been in Stubbs' comeback game at Easter Road.

The first time I met Stubbs he was just a few days into the job of Hibs manager. This was in Portobello – Edinburgh's Venice Beach, his home for the duration. Porty is a place of shifted sand – the seafront is partly-imported – but the man wasn't wobbling, despite the challenges facing him. The eighth boss in ten years, he was unperturbed by the post appearing a thankless task, a near-impossible one. The manager immediately before him presided over a horrific transmogrification of a Jekyll & Hyde nature – or a Preston North End 26, Hyde 0 nature – as they went from Euro hopefuls to relegation chumps. The manager before him had been responsible for monumental stinkers, the two worst results in the club's history.

Stubbs dominates the room but in a quiet way. He impresses with his determination but this is football, nothing more life-or-death than that: worse things happen to people than their teams failing to fulfil sometimes over-inflated aspirations. He repeats what he said on his first day in the job of wanting to make the supporters proud. The man has undoubted presence.

Stubbs' battles with cancer have left him with one fewer testicle and a scar from surgery, after which forty staples were needed to put him back together. 'They opened me up and moved various organs out and to the side to get to the tumour,' he told me. Cancer took Stubbs to 'the darkest, darkest places' and the pain was overwhelming. 'I could feel the staples, I could feel my insides, I could feel everything.'

He talked freely about all of this. 'I live with cancer,' he said. He spoke movingly of his dad Ronald who delivered cigarettes for a living but crucially drove the youngest of his five children to juvenile games in and around Kirkby, the Liverpool overspill which became a town, and who developed cancer at the same time as Stubbs and would eventually die of it. 'Dad told a friend of mine: 'I want to take all the cancer from Alan, take it with me so he'll be alright.' That was typical of him, selfless to the last.'

Stubbs made Ronald proud when he signed for Everton, the team they supported together, and during our chat that day he conveyed the sense he's striving to demonstrate his gratitude to his father for his football life. But this is not a tense or wound-up fellow; he has a 'carefree' air. That's down to having fought cancer and won. 'I live for each new day. What's the point in worrying?' Maybe other better-qualified candidates for the Hibs job were scared off by the high casualty rate but not Stubbs.

The cynic will say that having coached at Everton but never managed before, he's a cheap option for a club which doesn't like to splash the cash. If it's not working come the autumn he can be removed and an old hand in a dugout duvet shuffled into position. But there's something tantalising about the appointment: Stubbs hails from England's redoubtable north. He was a centre-back. He played for Celtic. Wasn't that Tony Mowbray, too? Mowbray's Hibs were a bonnie side; a similar model will be most welcome after much recent grimness.

Hibs, Hearts and Rangers, all fighting for the Championship title and automatic promotion, will make 2014-15 a second-tier season like no other in Scottish football history, and a far more cut-throat league than the Premiership. But Stubbs doesn't need presence in his first few breathless weeks in the job; just points. His goalie scores the winner in the opening game against Livingston and then the team lose three in a row, including the Edinburgh derby, never a smart thing to do.

Maybe the rookie deserves some sympathy. Stubbs took over with half the old squad having been invited to find new employment after demotion and those that remained still staggering around in shock. He had to find new players, his feet and a feel for the Scottish game – all at once and quickly. Then comes the first eye-catching result: a win at Ibrox. It's choreographed by Scott Allan, one of the new signings. An enormously talented attacking midfielder who's wasted a couple of years of his career, Allan suddenly starts demanding the ball for ninety minutes, reverse-passing teams to death and by the season's end will be Scottish football's hottest property. His manager is credited with the transformation; he says it's all down to the player.

Hearts get off to a flier and don't let up. Hibs are unlucky in the next two derbies and then they beat their city rivals. Rangers are thrashed at Easter Road, then Hibs win again at Ibrox. Hibs finish runners-up only for Rangers – by then on their third manager of the season – to find a way to squeeze them out in the playoffs. The promotion campaign has been a failure but in the final minutes of the final match applause ripples round Easter Road. The fans – among Scotland's grouchiest, grumbliest and hardest-to-please – don't normally greet non-achievement so warmly. Stubbs, though, has given them back their football team.

The Hibs way. Trapping it under a jam-jar is tricky, just as trapping the ball was tricky for some reluctant Easter Road legends down the years. Does it exist?

Hibs fans, obviously, think it does. They like the team to have flair; thus Hearts supporters sneeringly call them flairists. Actually, Jambos call Hibbies poncing delusional snobs and borderline-Nazi master-race purists who perpetuate a myth of Brazil-influencing attacking aesthetics and who have actually borne witness to some chronic rubbish down the years.

It's true; they have. But Hibs fans don't appoint the club's managers, or hand them scribbled notes before kick-off suggesting how best to bring about a total fitba afternoon. There are managers who will come along and decide Hibs should be tougher, more direct, more prosaic. All supporters want to see their team win but some place a slightly greater premium on winning with style. If your father was fortunate enough to witness the Famous Five, then if you and he were lucky enough to watch Turnbull's Tornadoes together, it's an inevitable and entirely permissible reaction when the ball is hoofed long and high to weep into your velvet sleeve, your snuff box or your first edition written by one of the French intellectuals.

Stubbs' predecessor was Terry Butcher. The faithful readied themselves for one of those eras where it was decreed the team would have to win ugly. Imagine how the fans felt, then, having to watch Hibs lose ugly. But they approve of Stubbs, his diamond formation, his charging wing-backs, his choice of Liam Fontaine as a ball-playing centre-back in the manager's own image, his trust in the creative workshop operated by Scott Allan and fellow midfielder Dylan McGeouch, his astute parenting of the young striker Jason Cummings to find a balance between responsibility and radgeness, increasing the boy's wisdom without compromising the fearlessness, and last but not least his wild-card pick – an example of that carefree nature, perhaps – of the occasional dazzle of Dominique Malonga. 'Stubbsy, Stubbsy,' chorus the fans, happy with their team again.

The Scottish Cup in 2014-15? Hibs receive favourable draws all the way to the semi-finals but that means Hampden where they usually lose. This defeat is the eleventh out of fifteen visits since the century began. So maybe Stubbs won't be able to overcome the hoodoo which has broken far more experienced men. Anyway, promotion is the main aim, isn't it?

*

Stubbs' second season starts like the first: slowly. Rangers want Scott Allan, table a couple of derisory bids, he eventually goes to Celtic, but Rangers benefit anyway because Hibs' preparations are disrupted.

This colours relations between Hibs and Rangers, two clubs who're never spliff-sharing Cheech & Chong at the best of times. Rangers are now managed by Mark Warburton, a former City trader and a feisty character easily wound up by Stubbs. Their exchanges ensure the Championship is no less fascinating for Hearts having left it. Plus, Falkirk's boss, Peter Houston, wants in on the mind games and wind-ups.

Stubbs has brought John McGinn from St Mirren and Liam Henderson on loan from Celtic to ensure the Hibs midfield is no less fascinating for Allan having left it. After losing their opening two matches, Hibs stay unbeaten for four months and are neck-and-neck with Rangers at the top of the Championship. In the League Cup there are handsome wins over Premiership opposition, Aberdeen and Dundee United. Hibs are playing with verve, the fans chant 'Stubbsy, Stubbsy', the second half of the season holds considerable promise but the man himself is keeping cool. You never see Stubbs roaring his head off, bouncing around on the touchline, reminding everyone he's the manager – and you certainly don't see him taking the acclaim when his song starts. He likes to stay in the dugout with a cup of coffee, only approaching the pitch at the end to shake the hands of the opposition players. The fans like Stubbs' style. They like his team's style, very much the Hibs way. As Christmas approaches I don't reckon the supporters are thinking about the Scottish Cup this season. The league is tense, all-consuming and vital. The cup, the bloody cup, can surely be put on hold. I mean, when the wait gets to 114 years, what's another one or two or ten?

The draw for the fourth round is made on 1 December. Hibs will start away to Raith Rovers. Stubbs says: 'The Scottish Cup is the Holy Grail, isn't it? Well, it can be won. Just ask Indiana Jones . . .'

FOUR

'HE JUMPED FROM SOMEWHERE AND SMICKED THE BALL AWAY'

'The future is bright with promise and the hope may be expressed that the team's little eccentricities will belong in the past, and that they will achieve fresh glories and add new lustre to the "ould name".'

WELL, THAT DIDN'T quite happen, did it?

The words come from the *Edinburgh Evening News* in its match report of Hibs' last Scottish Cup triumph. On 26 April, 1902 Hibernians, as they were known then, beat Celtic 1-0. When the trophy was presented to the team, Easter Road chairman Phil Farmer declared: 'We have attained our hearts' desire and I am the proudest man in Great Britain.'

The *Evening News* painted a picture of a club always striving, always in vain, and of the huge effort spent in trying to match their only other success in the tournament in 1887, and the relief and joy of this finally being achieved:

'Since that famous day at Hampden when Willie Groves flashed down the wing and enabled Pat Lafferty to outwit [Jimmy] McCauley, Dumbarton's great custodian, the Hibernians have travelled far and fared variously, and now that they stand on the highest pinnacle, those who stuck by them through the long and weary way may be well satisfied.'

Long? Weary? Fared variously? The delay in once again getting their hands on the trophy ending after a piddling fifteen years, Hibs would go on to prove them themselves world-class at faring variously in the cup and those little eccentricities would fester, balloon and suppurate, driving the people of Leith half-mad and resulting in a giant cross being painted on all entrances to the port, warning of a terrible plague. Not for nothing is Leith's motto Persevere, as in 'to continue in a course of action even in the face of difficulty or with little or no indication of success'.

Hibs must have been pleased it was Celtic they vanquished. The Hibees had been formed to keep young men from Edinburgh's Cowgate – 'Little Ireland' where survivors of the potato famines had sought a new life – out of the alehouses. The year after their first cup triumph they loaned players to Celtic, not yet properly established, and then had their best men poached by the Glasgow club.

Hibs' victorious manager in 1902 was Dan McMichael, Bobby Atherton was captain and the goal which would haunt his successors in green and white for 114 years was scored by Andrew McGeachan. The final was played at Celtic Park following the disaster at Ibrox – venue for the first finals of the new century – a few weeks before when a stand collapsed killing twenty-five spectators and the mood of the 16,000 crowd was sombre.

The game did little to lift their spirits. The *Evening News* wrote of the 'ghastly poverty' of the play, with the goalposts being viewed as 'superfluities' by the shot-shy forwards, and added: 'From beginning to end there was scarcely sufficient action to impact a tremor or quicken the beat of a single pulse.' The *Edinburgh Evening Dispatch* reckoned it 'the poorest final on record'.

That title was almost certainly grabbed by other finals which followed but fans of the victors are generally unperturbed by the non-classic tag, especially if their team have mustered a great effort and deserved to win, which was the case with Hibs that fabled year.

The defence was heroic and Robert Glen was the star man in this department for how 'in the nick of time [he] jumped from somewhere and smicked the ball away'. Even when 'cooped and cornered' he would 'resort to overhead kicks and trick football of the neatest kind'. Half-backs James Harrower and Bernard Breslin 'constituted a rock on which the Celtic attack was split into atoms'. Up front Patrick Callaghan 'worked like a Trojan' while McGeachan displayed 'capital dribbling powers'.

The breakthrough fifteen minutes from the end resulted from a corner. In Hibs' long and painful cup history, Callaghan's delivery would go down as the corner of the century. 'The ball dropped about the middle of the goal,' reported *The Scotsman*, 'Atherton jumped and let it pass, and McGeachan sent it between [Hugh] Watson and [Willie] Lonie into the net, [Robert] McFarlane not seeing it until it had passed the goal line.'

After a winners' reception at Glasgow's Alexandra Hotel, a 'hurricane of cheers' propelled the team's train back to Edinburgh. When they arrived at Haymarket Station, the tune was 'See the Conquering Hero Comes'. Newhaven Brass Band had been 'retained for eventualities', wrote the *Dispatch*, and then the bandsmen got into a brake which led the players' four-in-hand carriage for the procession along Princes Street and a 'demonstration of a most enthusiastic nature'.

Thousands crammed the thoroughfare and progress of other transport 'was indeed threatened'. At Register House the team were 'completely circled by a moving mass' and on the tramcars forced to a halt the people waved handkerchiefs and hats. '"Good old Hibs" was the cry on almost everybody's lips,' confirmed *The Scotsman*.

The four-in-hand inched down Leith Street. 'At London Road,' reported the *Evening News*, 'it was thought advisable to try to shake off the crowd, and for this purpose the horses were put into a sharp trot, but the spirit of the enthusiasts was too great.'

What a great day. These Hibs had been cooped. They'd been cornered. They thought they might have been cursed not to win the cup a second time. Their successors would dream of decisive corners and delirium on the streets and gridlock at Register House but every year this would be frivolous fantasy.

FIVE

'MIND WHERE YER PITTIN' YER FIT . . .'

9 January 2016
Raith Rovers 0 Hibernian 2

THE OPENING ROUND of the cup for the big boys – and even for less-than-studious types like Hibs who've been put back a year or two – usually happens in the first fortnight of January when it can stay gloomy all day, no one has any money left after Christmas and grounds like Raith Rovers' Stark's Park can seem even more careworn than usual.

And be just as deadly for the unsuspecting, the ill-prepared and, especially, the history-haunted.

Stark's Park looks, well, stark. Advertising for Blind Davy's – a shop selling blinds, presumably run by Davy, who may not be visually impaired – dwarfs the stadium's name on the front elevation. It is one day out from being exactly twenty-five years since I was last here and a great chunk of the terracing where I stood with my father has disappeared. In its place are a couple of metal boxes, the kind of windowless compartments you see on building sites where if the foreman and his five labourers were to pass wind simultaneously after Steak Bakes all round from Greggs, the stench might kill you. It is here that Alan Stubbs will come post-match to explain, in the event of a defeat, that the league was always the number one priority or, should Hibs win, that the cup's a nice bonus but promotion's the thing.

And that Stark's Park encounter a quarter of a century before? Oh, Hibs lost.

The team Stubbs has picked for the tie doesn't suggest an all-out targeting of the holy grail, the holey pail. There's no Jason Cummings, sparking rumours he might be sold in the transfer window, might even be on his way already, although it turns out he's unwell. In his place is Chris Dagnall, a striker who'd scuffed around England's lower divisions before a move to Kerala Blasters of the optimistic-sounding Indian Super League. Another short-term loanee making his debut is Norwegian defender Niklas Gunnarsson.

You wonder what Dagnall will make of Kirkcaldy. Perhaps surprisingly, there isn't a curry-house here called the Taj Mahal. And you continue to wonder what Dominique Malonga makes of Scotland, its physical, urgent football and seepingly damp winters. This is a French-born Congolese forward of delicious ability and dubious attention-span. Apparently constructed from pipe cleaners, he moves like a push-up wobbly toy. On his day he's unplayable. The other days he might as well not be playing.

This doesn't look like it's going to be his day. A snell wind had greeted Hibs fans as they crossed the Forth Bridge and piled off the train and into Fife's former centre of linoleum excellence. The incessant rain on the trudge from the train station had caused them to hug the sturdy garden walls of some fine mansions and it's not letting up. The Stark's Park DJ – a top comedian, for sure – will begin his song selection at the thoroughly drookit arena with the Beatles' 'Good Day Sunshine'.

But Kirkcaldy could probably make a claim for being Scotland's Beatle-town. The Fab Four songbook's only Scottish reference comes in Cry Baby Cry: 'The Duchess of Kirkcaldy always smiling/And arriving late for tea.' Kirkcaldy has never had a duchess; the woman in the song is thought to have been the wife of a local concert promoter who entertained John Lennon during a pre-fame tour of small towns. Now there's a pub called The Duchess of Kirkcaldy. In the afternoon dankness, the hostelry's Christmas lights, not yet taken down, send morse-code messages to oil platforms in the estuary which twinkle back, but the discerning football fan might choose to stick with the Penny Farthing, one of the finest watering-holes in the lower-league away-day gazetteer.

At the stadium, a steady climb from the waterfront, the sellers of the match programme are taking up their positions. Gordon Brown, the former Prime Minister, used to perform this function, as he'll remind you if invited to blether about his favourite team. Broon seems to be pushing hard for his programme-flogging to be included among the top three facts every football fan knows about Raith. At the moment these are: 1) The shipwrecking of the 1923 side off the Canary Isles; 2) The half-time score from 1995: Bayern Munich 0, Rovers 1; 3) TV results-man Sam Leitch's blithe ignorance of the club's whereabouts during the viddyprinter service: 'They'll be dancing in the streets of Raith tonight.'

But Hibs with that infernal cup curse make every other club's USP seem like whiny, attention-seeking piffle.

When the Hibees mucked up the 1958 final to Clyde, the dynamite-booted Joe Baker was probably expected to win it by himself only to be caught punching the ball into the Bully Wee net, I was one year old and happily oblivious of the hex. Over the next few years Hibs' cup record was fairly abysmal. Admittedly there were tough draws pitting them against the biggest teams – Celtic and Rangers, the Old Firm, who hogged the trophy – but when Hibs were presented with better opportunities, they blew them. In 1965, with the Old Firm posted missing in both league and cup, a wonderfully freakish season treasured by fans of Scotland's great diddy rump, Hibs reached the semi-finals. The stage seemed set for Willie Hamilton, their mystical midfielder. But Hammy, fond of nutmegs and also Bacardis, was the type who would be declared the silver salver-winning seven-goal man-of-the-match while on close-season tour in Canada, only to bend the plate over his knee so it fit in his holdall for the journey home. That's the legend, anyway. Three years after that defeat by Dunfermline Athletic, a side able to boast the ahead-of-his-time penalty-box ghost Peter Cormack, hip-swinging screamadelic pin-up winger Peter Marinello and thundering goal monster Colin Stein – before they all left Easter Road for big money – would lose timidly at Airdrieonians.

Preoccupied with the space race, cap guns, *Mad* magazine, *Monty Python, Rowan & Martin's Laugh-In*, my Swiss Army knife, spies and American Civil War bubblegum cards, I wasn't devastated by any of this. Football, Hibs and the Scottish Cup were still not dominating my world. And then suddenly they were.

The first time I saw the club play in the tournament was in March 1971, a home tie against Forfar Athletic. My father and I used stand at the foot of the old main terracing, a sizeable clump in a city of seven hills. Arthur's Seat, the extinct volcano from geography lessons, stood proud to the south-west but the terracing was a far more impressive peak. Dad and I had to climb into the clouds to get to the top, then drop down the other side to reach our favourite spot: twelve steps up from the touchline, to the right of halfway.

Even though this mountaineering soon became routine I remember stopping at the summit that cup afternoon and gazing at the pitch, which famously sloped in those days, and wondering if there really were recorded instances of footballers hurtling so fast down the gradient they briefly became airborne. That's what Dad told me. I stood next to a post supporting a loudspeaker and reckon I can tell you the name of the song that was a tinny and muffled delight – 'Tomorrow Night' by Atomic Rooster. (Okay, it might have been Clodagh Rodgers' 'Jack in the Box'). This was a crisp, clear afternoon in early spring, hinting at renewal and great possibilities. Then the opposition appeared for their warm-up, looking exactly like West Ham United on an awayday.

Despite their light blue garb with two claret bands across the chest, Forfar played like bridies. Then a division below Hibs when there were only two in Scotland, the team from Angus were tanked 8-1. Hibs didn't even need Joe Baker, who'd just returned to Easter Road in white boots and tremendous sideburns following sojourns to Italy and elsewhere. This Scottish Cup lark seemed quite easy.

It wasn't, of course, and Hibs would continue to fall to big teams – and wee teams. Maybe not Forfar but Raith Rovers have been ending Hibee interest in the cup for more than a century, winning in 1913, 1953 (4-1 in a second replay, despite the presence of four of the Famous Five), 1956, 1998 and as recently as 2014. But surely when it comes to the cup for the Hibees, every other team in Scotland is a potential jinx.

Terry Butcher, a blood-spattered stout yeoman hero of the England national team who became an adopted teuchter from his time in charge of Inverness Caley-Thistle, was the Hibs manager for the most recent Raith tie. I'd met him a few days before and he'd been in confident, expansive mood, discussing his love of Turner landscapes, Deep Purple riffs and the motivational techniques with which he was impressing conferences of corporate thrusters. But Butcher was undone by a stunning Raith back-header – it was every bit as good as that by West Germany's Uwe Seeler against England in the Mexico World Cup – and never recovered from the defeat. Hibs plummeted into the Championship which meant that for all their reputation as one of the biggest names in Scottish football, they were meeting Rovers as equal members of Scotland's second tier.

It's almost time for another cup odyssey to begin. This is the moment to scan the stadium, fix on something and remember it, just in case 2016 is to be *the* year. I mean, it doesn't seem like it will be the year. Stubbs is too inexperienced; the club must focus on the league. Still I need a souvenir, something which will remind me of rain-lashed January if by some crazy twist of fate there's to be sunshine in May. Then the Tannoy announcer obliges. During a small, late surge at the turnstiles by the stragglers from the pubs, he cautions: 'Mind where yer pittin' yer fit.'

The pitch looks gloopy. Maybe Hibs will have to take inspiration from David Bowie, who's just died, and be 'tigers on Vaseline'. They're in their purple away shirts. This is a second strip they've modelled occasionally, and one I'll always associate with forlorn trips to Parkhead in the first half of the 1970s, my father stomping out as the fifth Celtic goal hit the net followed by the anxious walk to our car, hoping it hadn't been raised on bricks because we'd declined to take up the toerag entrepreneurs on their unrepeatable offer: 'Watch yer motor, mister?' Raith, meanwhile, have again retired the classic two blue stripes across the chest, revived recently. That's a shame but in the early skirmishes they show themselves to be up for this tie.

Thanks goodness for Marvin Bartley, the unsentimental midfielder. Some teams are never without an enforcer; Hibs will only experiment with them now and again, perhaps in response to the charge that the club's overarching philosophy is shot through with wimpishness. Only silly snobs say these minders have no place at Easter Road because the best of them, like Matthias Jack from Alex McLeish's team of the early noughties, become folk-heroes. In the way he scatters the opposition like skittles in the middle of the park, Marvin Bargeley – or Marvin Bagatelle – is well on his way to that kind of status. Plus, being sentimental for a moment, he came to Hibs from Leyton Orient, a club for whom I've always had a soft spot for having the least glamour of all the London teams. Their old passport-sized match programmes were cute, too.

*

There's nothing between Hibs and Raith today. Familiarity – they played each other only the previous week in the league – has bred stalemate, a stodgy pie, with no shots on goal recorded in the first half. This is knockout football, of course, and it should be different. A welcome break from the divisional slog, a chance to cast off angst and doubt and play with freedom. For many clubs that's exactly what the cup is.

But Hibs are the only team whose cup form, or non-form, is a major issue. Every player, before every tie, will be asked about the curse, how it's now 114 years and counting, and why on earth they think they're going to be the guys who'll finally bring the trophy home. They'll be challenged on this, no matter their excellent form at that moment or their ignorance of history. They must answer for a century-plus of cup disavowal, despair and disaster.

The new boys Dagnall, ex-Orient too, and Gunnarsson have barely been Hibees for 114 minutes and look well short of sharpness. Hibs fans might already have been thinking: 'Ach, maybe not this year.' Meanwhile the Raith diehards in the old Main Stand – wooden seats, quirky, bends round a corner flag – will be fancying they could take the tie.

Stark's Park hunkers close to the East Coast Main Line and is one of the world's great grounds viewable from railway tracks. You could almost jump off your train and land on the roof of what used to be the Railway Stand, now the Key-Tech. The Hibbies are housed here and behind the far goal in another structure with a good story attached.

The McDermid Stand is named after the top Scottish crimewriter and Rovers fanatic Val McDermid who helped the club when they were broke so these plastic pop-up seats have effectively been paid for by blood, guts, torture, dismemberment and ever more elaborate murder. She stresses that this dedication is shared with her late father Jim who was the stadium's turnstile manager for many years and discovered the greatest-ever Rover, Jim Baxter, but McDermid is pretty special: there can't be too many gay, football-loving whodunnit practitioners in Fife.

She once told me of a Kingdom derby against East Fife where her son by artificial insemination was the mascot: 'The announcer asked Cameron who he'd brought to the game and – bless him – he uttered words never used before at the Rovers: "My mum and my stepmum."' Did the away end jeer? 'Well, East Fife, don't forget are from Methil where they're slow on the uptake. By the time they'd worked out our domestic arrangements the moment to hurl abuse was gone.'

It wouldn't be a crime, the Hibs fans must be thinking, if the home side were to win by dint of a rubbishy goal. That's how the Scottish Cup has gone for their team. Raith Rovers, at Stark's Park, with the lead piping – a hoary outcome to make us groan, then pack the board away for another year.

This one is starting to resemble a 1987 tie at Clydebank – the Kilbowie Pleasuredome – which I still can't believe Hibs lost, although I shouldn't have been surprised. The team featured John Collins, Mickey Weir and Alan Rough. Seven days before Hibs had thrashed the Bankies in the league, scoring four goals. As *The Scotsman* reported, 'Clydebank were one of those sides put into the same league as Hibs expressly to make life a little easier for them'. It wasn't as if the opposition had suddenly and sneakily re-signed their greatest-ever, Davie Cooper, for a one-off star turn – simply that the strange paralysis which afflicts the Hibees in the cup had returned. Clydebank weren't better than Hibs in the cup game but one goal was always going to be enough to give them victory. Some of the Hibees' defeats during the hoodoo have come at places which no longer exist, including Airdrie's Broomfield, Third Lanark's Cathkin Park where Hibs' greatest-ever, Gordon Smith, took his final bow in 1959 – and Kilbowie.

*

Admittedly Raith don't seem to have an obvious candidate for the decisive strike today. There's no Joe Baker who, after Hibs, was just as prolific for Rovers. He scored goals everywhere, the antithesis of the striker who explains away a succession of sclaffs and duffs on the fact – and these words are uttered – that it can take a whole season for a player to settle at a new club.

But Raith surely won't need Baker to condemn Hibs to at least one more year of waiting. The cup simply isn't a happy competition for the club. It's an absolutely bloody tragic one and the fans must be sensing an all too familiar dénouement. Raith could probably bring on McDermid, the self-confessed 'big, old fat lezza', and she'd bounce the ball off her backside to nick it for them.

And then just after the hour-mark Hibs score. Darren McGregor, who'd replaced the wheezing Gunnarsson moments earlier, sees the ball come all the way across to him from Lewis Stevenson on the left and it's seriously inviting a thwack. If he feels the weight of history on his shoulders, to say nothing of the weight of being a defender still working his way into the tie or the weight of the next goal for Hibs in the Scottish Cup being their 1,000th, it doesn't show in his thumping low finish.

McGregor came to Easter Road at the start of the season, having been discarded by Rangers, but he won't have been oblivious to recent calamities in the cup and elsewhere as he grew up a Hibs fan. His enjoyment at playing for his boyhood heroes shows in his gutsy performances in the centre of defence and, on days like today, when he has to motor forward from wing-back.

Stevenson on the other hand experienced those traumas first-hand. To this generation of Hibee, the scoreline 0-7 has a different meaning: the worst defeat suffered by a Scottish club in Europe. Stevenson, converted from midfield to wing-back, played in the mauling by Malmo. But that isn't quite the club's worst result. In the 2012 cup final Hibs were beaten 5-1 by Hearts and Stevenson experienced that one, too. After eleven seasons of these kind of hardcore losses surely the guy deserves a break.

If McGregor's goal was a good one, Hibs' second and clincher three minutes later is even better. Malonga – remember how this wasn't supposed to be his kind of dank afternoon? – collects the ball in the middle of the park twenty yards out following another surge down the left by the ever-willing Stevenson. He takes one stride because when you're big, daft Dom in a dwam, that's all you reckon to be necessary. The shot zings into the top left-hand corner of the net. 'Oh oh oh, Dominique Malonga,' sing the Hibs fans, to the tune of Black Lace's prog-rock classic, 'Do the Conga'. Malonga is frequently infuriating but now and again the fancy takes him and this goal is a real collector's item for the devotees of his occasional whimsy who the rest just think weird. None of us know this but it will be his last strike for Hibs and he'll soon return to the balmier enclaves of Italy's second tier.

The tie is won but not without a struggle. It certainly isn't appropriate to shriek, in the manner of a famous Norwegian TV commentator: 'Val McDermid! Gordon Brown! Jim Baxter! Sam Leitch! The Duchess of Kirkcaldy! Your boys took a helluva beating!' In the Penny Farthing afterwards, some Hibbies think about launching into their Malonga ditty again, but in a pub full of signed photos of showbiz troupers, including Harry Worth, Dickie Henderson and Matt Munro, that doesn't seem right either. Indeed if these guys were still alive, the Hearts songbook interspersed with jokes about Hibs and the Scottish Cup would have kept them in regular bookings in west Edinburgh, the package-tour finishing up at the Gorgie Suite, a kind of Talk of the Toon for boys in maroon.

Hibs' chronic aversion to the cup has become a music hall joke that's outlasted the tradition of music halls. They've only succeeded in winning their first game in this year's competition, toiling through it for long enough. Let's not get carried away. See who we get in the next round. Major on the league.

Two days later the draw is made. Hibs are last out of the metaphorical hat in a competition they haven't won since men wore hats all the time, probably even in the bath and at bed-time.

It's Hearts away.

SIX

'I KNEW SOMETHING WAS FUNDAMENTALLY WRONG . . .'

IF HIBS HAD been in a better place in the summer of 2014 – rather than the basket-case Alan Stubbs inherited with only six players on the books and Alloa Athletic's drastic plastic and the Tony Macaroni Arena looming – then he doesn't think he'd have got the job.

'I was a risk,' he tells me. 'When I walked into Easter Road I didn't appreciate the scale of the task.' Maybe the club hierarchy didn't either, he reckons, and that if they had, perhaps a more experienced man would have been summoned. 'I knew something was fundamentally wrong, but I didn't realise the magnitude of the problem. But if the club knew I was a risk then credit to them for taking it.'

This might make the appointment sound like the equivalent of a hospital pass, but Stubbs is an optimistic fellow who didn't read it that way. Hibs were a famous old name. The post was a fantastic opportunity. Build the club back up and who knows what might be possible?

We meet in Liverpool in July 2016 when he's got a couple of days at home before the season gets under way at his new club, Rotherham United. He picks me up from Lime Street Station in his club car, parks the white BMW in a multi-storey and we walk past Liverpool Cathedral where fellow Scousers greet the strapping fellow in jeans, short-sleeve shirt and natty blue suede shoes, one of them quipping: 'Well done on winning that cup, Stubbsy!'

The scale of the job. The magnitude of the problem. What was it? 'I think that around football clubs there can be a mindset: "It would only happen to us." Maybe a lot of that at Hibs came from the outside. They're fated, they're doomed, whatever. But I definitely got it from the players and the staff as well. Whether it was the league, the cups, anything: "It wouldn't happen to anyone else, it would only happen to us."'

So how does a manager change that mentality? 'Winning games of football is a good start and as you go along hopefully the players start to trust you, start to believe in what you're trying to do.' He needed to find half a team and quickly, but the players had to be of a certain type.

'I was very conscious that they should be good players. That might seem obvious: no manager actively seeks out bad players. What I mean is they had to suit the football club. We – my coaches and I – did our research. We looked at the traditions of Hibs. This is a club where the supporters like to see guys get the ball down and be creative. They like the team to be pleasing on the eye: attacking, brave, expressive. That's what I wanted to give them: good footballers, hungry footballers, Hibs footballers.'

We talk about three of them: John McGinn, Liam Henderson and Scott Allan, who the previous day Stubbs had enticed to Rotherham on loan from Celtic. 'Football has its rogues, some are loveable and to me Scott just needed cajoling,' he says. 'He'd got a good move from Scotland down to West Brom and probably thought he was travelling upwards on this conveyor belt, forgetting about what got him onto it in the first place. When he came to us he was a bit lost but you could see his talent right away.'

Stubbs was disappointed to lose Allan and his flair but 'football doesn't wait for you, you have to respond'. He sounded out Celtic personnel about Henderson and especially the captain, Scott Brown. 'Scotty told me about a really good footballer with an exceptional attitude and that if we had the ability to get him we should. And John was a really big statement for us. St Mirren were looking for £100,000 and there were very few clubs in Scotland who would have been willing to pay that.'

With these three Stubbs acquired a reputation for getting the best out of young players, enabling talent to bud. If this is a skill, he says, then it comes from his hard-working parents in a tough community who 'always thought the best of you and wanted the best for you'. His father, not a football man as such, was the biggest influence on his career. 'He was the one at my side wherever I went. If I had to be out the house at six a.m. for a juvenile match, Dad was up at half-five: 'Come on, son, we're going.' Or me and my brother Ronnie would take a ball down to Windy Harbour in Kirby and kick it about for hours in all weather and Dad would be perched on the wall at the top end, dead understated, just watching.'

But Stubbs stresses that Henderson and McGinn weren't in any way lost. 'John was only going one way in his career, and the same with Liam. John was thinking about playing in America, he had offers. That tells you I think that he's got a strong mentally. And Liam is a boy with an opinion. Not in a negative way; he fully believes in himself and knows what he wants to do.'

Obviously promotion was the main aim. Return the club to the Premiership, that was the brief. 'No one mentioned the Scottish Cup, the 113 years as it was then, and to be honest I didn't really know about the so-called jinx when I arrived.' So how long before it was mentioned? 'Oh, a while. Maybe half an hour . . .'

Away to Raith Rovers was a tough opener. 'It could have been one of those cup runs which ends in a whimper. That happens to clubs sometimes and I dare say it's happened to Hibs in the past. But we got over our sticky start to that game.'

Interestingly he forgets the score, forgets that Hibs scored two that day. Maybe that's the effect Dominique Malonga can have. 'One week Dom would be sublime but the next he wouldn't look up for the match and I'd want the opposition to kick him early, just to wake him up. It didn't bother me if he got a kick because usually there would be a positive reaction – 'You'll never do that again because you won't get near me' – and he'd burst into life. I know he divided the fans but I think all of them appreciated he had skills which should be allowed to flourish at a club like Hibs. We persevered with him but Dom never stays anywhere longer than two years and we were fortunate to get the year and a bit we did when he scored some lovely goals.'

No such problems with the attitude of the other Stark's Park scorer. Darren McGregor is like the fan who wins a quiz in the match programme – Q: How many times have Hibs lost a Scottish Cup final since their last triumph? A: Nine, and don't we know it – with the prize a run-out in the team. 'That's him,' laughs Stubbs. 'It's vital, and especially these days given the transient nature of football, that you have guys who're in touch with the community and know what the club's all about because they were the kids on the terraces who dreamed of being out there on the park. I had a few like that at Hibs and Darren was one of them. In the dressing-room you could see how much Hibs meant to him when we won – and when we lost.'

SEVEN

VALE OF TEARS

WHAT'S IN A name? There's a lot, dammit, wrapped up in Heart of Midlothian. The old site of the parliament and the town council. A place where once stood a prison and a hangman's scaffold. Sir Walter Scott's finest novel. A target for the good-luck gobbing of brilliant legal minds and gentlemen of leisure. It's a lovely name, too.

So is Queen of the South who must have one of the bonniest situations in all football. A glance at the Lowther Hills confirms you've travelled far from the Central Belt. A glance at the attractive jumble of spires and roofs beyond the Terregles Street End makes you think you might be in a Tuscan town. Look left and there's the Hole i' the Wa' End, where indeed there's a hole in the wall for the serving of pies. If you're seeing all of this you'll be in the old wooden stand at Palmerston Park and any second now the Byrdsian jingle-jangle of the Queens' theme tune will start up. Lovely.

But what do we think of Vale of Leven Old Church Old Boys' Association? Maybe it's too long, with the clunkiness of a repeated word, to challenge the big two but charming all the same. Their time was the 1930s, as a kind of corner flag-of-convenience for Vale of Leven. The three-times Scottish Cup-winners had got into bother with the SFA for failing to fulfill a fixture so this lot competed in the tournament in the years before the Second World War.

In 1936 the Old Boys stood in the way of yet another Hibs' tilt at the trophy. Beaten by some bent-double beadles and long-serving caretakers with big bunches of keys for every cranny and crypt? Some sado-masochistic Hibbies might have fancied that for the record books, surely the biggest humiliation in an overflowing cup-load of failure.

Vale Ocoba, as they were called, had home advantage. According to the *Edinburgh Evening News'* man at Milburn Park, Alexandria they were 'as game as fighting-cocks and to give them their due had the Easter Road XI on the run at times'. Hibs prevailed, however, eventually winning 3-1. So not only does glory elude the Hibees, they can't even manage a spectacular defeat.

They tried hard. 'One of the most sombre, most disastrous days,' was the *Edinburgh Evening Dispatch's* reaction to Cowdenbeath's 3-0 win in 1927. The 1920s amounted a strange decade. Two finals reached, but that slump in Fife and one at Armadale among the early departures. Talk about perverse.

In the 1950s, though, Hibs surely became the world champs of obstinacy and obliqueness. The decade featured the most first-round defeats and yet this was the era of the Famous Five, title triumphs, record crowds, floodlighting innovation, conquistadoring football, the inaugural European Cup adventure and Brazilian tours.

Ah, Brazil. I picked up the ball and ran across the beach with it. When told, mouth agape in awe, about the Hibees guest-starring in the Maracana in 1953, I was quickly fantasising about the team being the blueprint for Pele and Carlos Alberto's World Cup-winners seventeen years later. Maybe it was more than that: did Hibs not in fact discover the great land? Perhaps Rio's Sugar Loaf Mountain was a man-made construction homaging the old Easter Road slope. Perhaps the inspiration for Lola, the showgirl in Barry Manilow's prog-rock classic 'Copacabana', was an exotic dancer at a Leith Docks social club flaunting a 'Persevere' tattoo on her left bumcheek. But the sad truth is that in the fabulous, frontiering 50s, exits from the Scottish Cup totalled an infamous five.

In 1950, reported the *Dispatch*'s J.F. Barclay, 'Hibs' pressure was almost unbelievable but nothing it seems could beat this wonder-man guarding the Thistle goal' (Partick's Bobby Henderson). Three years later they lost to Aberdeen. 'Here they were at last,' groaned the press-box's Bob Scott, 'with the best chance in years to bring cup joy to Edinburgh and they threw it away with some of the most insipid and futile stuff I have ever seen them play.'

In 1955 the hacks were asking: 'Why no boy-star Jackie Plenderleith?' Hearts duly thumped their capital neighbours 5-0. The following year the *Dispatch*'s Bill Heeps penned the Famous Five's obituary like this: 'Phfft went the brightest flame in post-war Scottish football in Kirkcaldy yesterday as Hibs, a very jaded Hibs, slumped out of the Scottish Cup.'

I didn't know the Five had such a strong aversion to the competition until opening up the programme for the 1987 tie at Clydebank at the 'Spotlight on our visitors' page. My father, who worshipped the glorious forward-line, had neglected to mention their great flaw, probably so as not to disillusion me any more than Hibs were doing right at that moment.

Looking at those years when the club hardly made a dent in the competition, it's difficult to detect a pattern. They would run into trouble when required to play Celtic and Rangers but often fared no better against the other Glasgow teams, Partick Thistle, Third Lanark and Clyde, the latter bringing to a juddering end a week-long carnival of celebration following the Vale Ocoba triumph (joke).

Raith Rovers have frequently put Hibs out of their misery, but not as often as Aberdeen – twelve times in all, a pattern for sure. And then there are Hearts, methodically testing the noose and trapdoor so they're ready to take down those ridiculous cup fantasists at the next opportunity.

The heaviest defeat was the 9-1 thrashing from Dumbarton in 1890. This was partial revenge for the Sons for what would become a dubious distinction in Scottish football: losing a Scottish Cup final to Hibs. Dumbarton would eventually share this with Celtic and no one else. Obviously Hibs' triumph of 1887, a 2-1 victory at Hampden, didn't begin a golden era. They quickly reverted to type and – euphemism alert – were able to concentrate on the league. Hearts beat them the following season and Mossend Swifts from the shale-mining West Lothian village did the honours next. Then they warmed up for the disaster at Dumbarton with a 6-2 skelping from Paisley's Abercorn.

Celtic and Rangers are Scotland's biggest clubs so in the cup they've always had furthest to fall and, notwithstanding those tankings way back in the 19th century, Hibs have never quite managed to suffer a defeat which has echoed down the years like Berwick Rangers' dumping of Rangers in 1967 and Inverness Caley-Thistle inspiring the headline 'Super Caley Go Ballistic Celtic Are Atrocious' after evicting the other half of the Old Firm from the competition in 2000.

But every decade that's passed there has always been at least one utterly dismal result, a howler among the routine losses. In 1977 *The Scotsman*'s Ian Wood reckoned the odds on Arbroath embarrassing Hibs must have been on a fantastical par with the Angus side achieving that world-record scoreline in the Scottish Cup – 36-0 against Bon Accord in 1885. But it happened; Arbroath won and deservedly so.

In 1984 the same paper's Mike Aitken noted that East Fife's Bayview, with its floodlights' span not quite extending to the goalmouths, provided 'a general atmosphere designed to cause the visiting team acute anxiety'. None were more anxious than the Hibees regarding the gloom-shrouded penalty-boxes.

Perhaps Jack Vettriano, an East Fife fan, was inspired to paint film-noirish imagery in later life having watched Methil night games as a boy. Then there's John Burnside's 'dark, dripping woods'. They come from the poet's memoir, referring to land behind his childhood home in Cowdenbeath, but a better description of Bayview you couldn't find.

Looking again at my match programme, the front cover probably offered a clue as to how to the night was going to pan out: it's a photo of the Hibs team which has been dreadfully underexposed. The Hibees didn't enter either goalmouth with purpose and a 'shambolic' performance produced the inevitable result.

In 1992 Airdrieonians were 'abysmal', according to one report, but Hibs were much worse. For the final staging of the competition in the twentieth century, it was Stirling Albion's turn to swing the axe, the winning goal in 1999 coming from Chris Jackson, who was twelve years at Easter Road and devastated at being released. 'It's a fairytale,' he said of the decisive strike. For Hibs it was a scarytale. They were stuck in the dark, dripping woods, scared of their own shadows, scared of life, scared of something much bigger than that: the Scottish Cup. 'They've been humiliated; they should be ashamed,' raged manager Alex McLeish that day.

In 114 years Hibs have spread their defeats around. They've given hope to just about everyone. They've been a great charity and great socialists, just not a great cup team.

Still, Vale Ocoba turned out to be all gas and no gaiters and were seen off without much fuss.

EIGHT

'HE'S BETTER THAN ZIDANE . . .'

7 February 2016
Hearts 2 Hibernian 2

COMEDIANS MUST HATE it when ordinary members of the public try to tell them jokes. Ronnie Corbett, who got to the age of eighty-five before he died, surely had to endure lots of rotten gags delivered by crashingly unfunny people. But I know he liked the one about Hibs, their Scottish Cup curse and the Polish goalkeeper.

'Hey Ronnie,' I said, 'these two Hibs fans are trudging away from Hampden, their team having just been skelpted four to nothing by Hearts, not a good day for their goalkeeper from Eastern Europe. One of them says to the other: "Christ, Jimmy, there are 20,000 Poles in Edinburgh and we huv tae be sent the one who's nae good with his hands."'

The keeper was Zbigniew 'Zibi' Malkowski, beaten on his near post for the second goal in the 2006 semi-final and fairly clodhopping regarding the third as well. Corbett, son of an Edinburgh master-baker, was a Hearts fan.

'Oh that's very good,' he chuckled when we met in Gullane, East Lothian, where he had a summer house. 'Yes, I like that.' And I have to tell you that all the signifiers of a joke enjoyed were in place: Ronnie was sat in a big chair and in danger of being swallowed up by it as, clasping his knees in merriment, his tiny, shiny tassel-loafered feet lifted clean off the floor.

There's a neat symmetry here, payback for the first gag I heard uttered in a theatre which was properly understood, gigglesomely enjoyed. Ronnie was in pantomime with Stanley Baxter at Edinburgh's King's Theatre, and in my memory this was the *Heaven's Gate* of yuletide entertainments, a bombastic, budget-smashing indulgence, with Ron and Stan as Cinderella's Ugly Sisters being lowered from the top of the proscenium arch by hot-air balloon expressly so that Ron, carrying a fine set of antlers, could quip: 'These are for Hearts – they need a few points.'

Corbett died in March 2016, hanging on just long enough for the 'Hibsing it' application to the *OED*, a modern joke at the expense of those cup-shy men in green and white. This was quite a year for big deaths: David Bowie, Muhammad Ali, Prince and Ronnie – Little Ron Corbett. He was still around for this tie, the 310th Edinburgh derby in the storied history of a fixture stretching back 140 years. It's being played at Tynecastle, not far from the old McVittie and Price biscuit factory where his dad earned a crumb.

*

The bus from the People's Republic of Leith to Gorgie, the Jambo domain, is a No 25. An alternative tourist guide, respectful of 1970s culture, might point out the Army & Navy Stores where Second World War gas-mask satchels were purchased as school-bags then immediately daubed with the names of your football team and favourite prog-rock groups. The guide would mention the Bandparts record shop, sadly no more, which didn't sell too much prog but where you went to commune at the listening-booths with the freaks and the skivers. Then the site of the kinetic sculpture, a Cremola Foam-tanked four-year-old's abandoned Meccano tower which was supposed to change colour in the harsh east wind but never really worked properly. Then on the climb to Princes Street another lost emporium, Cowan Tailoring, suppliers of Levi Sta-Press trousers, Ben Sherman checked shirts and College V jerseys because you liked glam-rock too.

At the other end you might get off a stop early to pay homage to a landmark of West Edinburgh. No, not the municipal shunkies at Ardmillan, but across the road, the site of the old Tivoli cinema, scene of many an ultra-violent shoot-em-'up. Other capital picture-houses showed westerns but in my memory they were a speciality of the most westerly one. At this frontier flea-pit I witnessed scalpings, poor varmints buried up to their necks in the sand and token women forced to swallow their own jewellery – these oaters were stoaters. The gruesome struggle between cowboys and indians was deemed suitable material by my parents for birthday treats – an era of more relaxed parenting, for sure.

If you felt claustrophobic after one of those flicks – and the suffocation was understandable – then stepping back out onto Gorgie Road and walking the last few hundred yards to Tynecastle wouldn't remove this sensation. The place is still like that now. While many football clubs have decamped to the modern prairies that are out-of-town developments on reclaimed land, Hearts have stayed hemmed in and hugger-muggered by tenements, factories, industrial yards, grand lodges, graveyards, grot, snot, ordinary life (and death). The express purpose of Tynecastle is to make you, the visiting fan, feel uncomfortable. Like you can hardly breathe. Like you're being force-fed, not diamonds and pearls, but a burnt pie. Or a maroon scarf, tangled up from being twirled, a fine Jambo tradition.

The Hearts song states: 'Auld Reekie supports them with pride.' Auld Reekie has two clubs but only one get the shout: 'Come on, the Edinburgh team!' The best that Hibs can hope to be called here is 'the wee team' and right now the Tynecastle faithful can claim the diminished status is official: Hearts, in the Premiership, are a full division above their internecine nearest-and-dearest.

How deep is my unlove? The rivalry is fierce – not as fierce as that between Celtic and Rangers, but Hibs and Hearts can cheerfully survive without the title of the greatest derby in football if owning it requires you to be a bigoted balloon. But the relationship between the fans is certainly more fiery than the one described in the programme for the 1958 cup-tie between the teams: 'Schoolboy chums, youths, men and young women, all pals, wearing different team ties, scarves and rosettes – is there any parallel in Great Britain?'

Some of my oldest friends are Jambos, though, and no fan of Hibs' brilliance in the 1950s like my father could have been unaware of Hearts' brilliance in the same decade. Dad told me about the Terrible Trio – Alfie Conn, Willie Bauld and Jimmy Wardhaugh, then introduced me to the latter when he worked as a BBC Scotland press officer in the old studios in the capital's Queen Street. Dad told me about Dave Mackay and what a thrill it was to meet the great warrior before he died. As dapper man as you'd expect of the proprietor of Dave Mackay Ties, possibly football's first star endorsement, he reminisced about sneaking into Tynecastle to watch his heroes by rolling under a big iron gate. Soon he was starring for Hearts, strengthening that famous barrel chest by bouncing it off fellow hard-man John Cumming who'd charge at him from the other end of Tynecastle's fabled brown gymnasium, where generations of players were toughened for the task of winning derbies.

All too quickly there came the dramatic evening when Mackay's parents, afraid of their newly-installed telephone and unable to comprehend why anyone would ring during Sunday Night at the London Palladium, had to field the call summoning him to Spurs. My father never saw Barney Battles Jr play but thought his story worth recounting: born after his father died, trailblazer of 1920s US soccer, Hearts hero, eleven goals against Hibs in three local cup finals in three weeks, masseuse, journalist, Newhaven publican and a jaunty name only equalled in Scottish football by his old man, Barney Battles Sr.

*

The very first all-Edinburgh meeting, on Christmas Day, 1875 was won by Hearts and their fans have claimed dominance from that day. The truth is that Hibs with the Famous Five won titles in the 1950s while Hearts and their Terrible Trio won cups. Hibs, thanks to that 7-0 apotheosis, rooled OK in the 1970s but then came a long unbeaten Hearts runs which drove Hibs mad. All of this – plus Hearts 4, Hibs 0 in 2006, plus an even greater Scottish Cup humiliation inflicted on the Hibees six years later – is remembered and re-told in an overblown Baz Luhrmann stylee by both sets of fans as they return to work alongside each other on Monday mornings to keep this bonnie town thrumming.

It's a raw February day, ideal conditions for a cup-tie and especially a derby. Most of the Hearts players sport gloves, the big jessies, although Alan Stubbs and the Hearts manager Robbie Neilson have shunned the dugout duvets, the latter being far too trendy for such comical outerwear. With the Hibs contingent crammed into the School End and Jambo supremacists filling the rest of the stadium, we've congregated at Sunday lunchtime to suit TV. But this doesn't dampen the atmosphere or quell the essential radgeness. Denied regular league skirmishes right now, the fans are intent on making the most of this face-time opportunity.

Frost forms on the quaint abuse and fierce banter as soon as words leave mouths. 'In your Gorgie slums!' 'We only won 5-1!' 'SHITE football team!' 'Paedo! Paedo!' 'Fuckin' fenian terrorist-lovin' bastard!' The last, spat by a shaven-headed Jambo with neck tattoos, is directed at Anthony Stokes, Hibs' new loan signing from Celtic and one of the most elusive and exasperating characters in Scottish football.

When he's in the mood Stokes can be a lethal striker but the fancy doesn't always take him. Hibbies know about his prowess better than most. Six seasons previously, aged twenty-one, the Irishman blazed into Easter Road, hit twenty-two goals and blazed out again. 'The greediest player I've ever seen,' opined upfront partner Derek Riordan, 'and coming from me that's saying something.' The switch to Celtic seemed to be developing him as a player when, in the 2013 Scottish Cup final, he traumatised his old club and earned man-of-the-match for laying on goals for others.

But he hasn't matured enough at Celtic, or exploited his talents to the full. He kept bad company, was friendly with Dublin mobsters, attended a benefit night for the family of an executed Real IRA leader and was reprimanded by the club. Then came regime change at Celtic Park and a stricter code for strikers: eat right, tackle back, be ready to run naked right through a Norwegian winter. Stokes dropped out of the picture.

Now he and Stubbs hope his return to Hibs will be mutually beneficial. If he can fire the club to promotion – still the top target – then he might force his way into the Republic of Ireland squad for Euro 2016. But there are obvious risks. What will his attitude be like? This is a settled side, doing pretty well – might he be disruptive?

The first thing we notice about Anthony Stokes, second time around, is his hair transplant. Very *Peaky Blinders*. The second thing is that he's retained the instinct of knowing precisely where to turn up in the penalty-box to cause the most fear and alarm. The third – understandably – is that he's rusty having spent a long time on the bench studying the match programme. So long he knew the page devoted to fans' offensive behaviour warnings – left unread by thousands – off by heart.

It's a fair old game in which to be trying to get yourself up to speed, one where players crave a first, reassuring touch of the ball like boozers need that nerve-calming drink as soon as the pub opens. Local lads Darren McGregor and Paul Hanlon of Hibs and Hearts' Sam Nicholson and Callum Paterson, who will have friends and family from what they term the dark side taunting them for months if they lose, tear into their challenges. They want to win their Barney Battles. The Scottish boys new to Embra hostilities catch up when the game hits the 100mph mark, which doesn't take long at all. The English and foreign players achieve optimum derby intensity soon after.

Tynecastle, though, isn't strange to this season's Hibee recruits, the team having played there just eight days previously in the League Cup semi-final against St Johnstone, an excellent victory. The fans had the run of the place, being allowed into areas which are out of bounds to them on derby days including the old main stand, a decrepit structure with a corrugated roof, wooden seats and leg-room dating from when the average Scottish male measured 5ft 4ins and was probably suffering from rickets. The invaders relished staking out their territory and among those stomping all over the Wheatfield Stand were a bunch of jolly japesters sporting home-made nuclear fallout onesies with 'Gorgie Survival Suit' scrawled on the back along with dust-masks and bearing signs warning 'Fragile roof'.

Today the Hibs midfield of John McGinn, Dylan McGeouch and Liam Henderson, with almost as much cockiness, are trying to take over the pitch. That victory over St Johnstone, in the harsh old-school terminology of football journalism, was a 'scalp' for the Hibees, Saints being the third Premiership side they've vanquished this season. The Comanches at the Tivoli would be impressed. Hearts, though, have no intention of allowing it to become four, rather fancying their chances this year in what the big team rather predictably call the 'big cup'. And when playmaker McGeouch is forced off injured after half an hour the tie starts to turn in the Jambos' favour.

Arnaud Djoum scores a goal which he'll probably never better in his career. The ball travels like a guided missile, staying a steady two feet off the ground, which is possibly more aesthetically-pleasing than a shot which zooms into the top corner. Bobby Charlton used to hit them like this, so did Italy's Marco Tardelli in the 1982 World Cup final. Nicholson nets a cheeky second soon after, delivering a 'Right up yez' gesture to the Hibs fans who're stunned by the turnaround.

*

Hibs' Scottish Cup record against Hearts isn't special. In the early years of both clubs' existence they met in the competition quite often; there weren't many other teams around. Maybe for Hibs the delirious peak was the mid-1880s when they won three ties in a row, the last of them 5-1 on the way to lifting the cup in 1887, the only other occasion bar you-know-when that the trophy has come to Leith.

Hibs would lose in the 1896 final to Hearts, a game played in Edinburgh at Logie Green. The venue was just a goal kick from my secondary school where, in voices not yet broken, boys would conduct impassioned arguments over which club had the superior floodlights and the stoutest terracing wall. Hibs emerged victorious from the game in 1912 then wouldn't win another capital tie until 1958. There were two defeats in the 1930s and in 1955 a 5-0 hammering.

The eighteen-year-old Joe Baker scored all Hibs' goals in that '58 tie, a 4-3 triumph marking the emergence of 'Scotland's first rock 'n' roll footballer'. Baker would move to Torino, hitting a statue in his brand-new Alfa Romeo, with Italian newspapers noting how the player failed to dribble round the great revolutionary Giuseppe Garibaldi, but at Tynecastle he had no difficulty negotiating the Hearts' defence, and no need for a sports car. Greased-up hair, grease-lightning on the pitch, Baker would also bang nine cup goals past Peebles Rovers but still couldn't help Hibs win the trophy.

The Edinburgh foes reconvened in the competition in 1966, Hearts victorious, and five years later, again at Tynie, I witnessed my first Edina-exclusive tie. This was also my first glimpse of Baker, back at Hibs for another spell, veteran class but still quick in the head, who left the running to the likes of Arthur Duncan. It was said of this flying left-winger, somewhat unkindly, that if the gates at the end he was hurtling towards weren't shut he'd race straight through, but such is the mythology surrounding Duncan's stupendous winning goal that day that fans reckon he was outside the stadium when he started his mazy dribble. Yardage, maybe even mileage, was added to it every time the goal was recalled. Did his slaloming through the Gorgie bustle of shoppers and drunks begin halfway up Robertson Avenue at Ronnie Corbett's old man's biscuit factory? Or was Duncan running so fast because he was being pursued by tomahawk-wielding braves from the Tivoli?

*

Two-nil down in the latest cup derby, Hibs are forced to re-organise again early in the second half because of an injury to the captain, David Gray. Right at this moment you might wonder if the Scottish Cup is beginning to drift from the minds of Stubbs and his players. They're already through to one final and, anyway, promotion's the biggie. Who needs the hassle of the holey pail? Who needs three more rounds of tedious questions about 114 years? The cup is just too damned elusive, the quest for it too bloody jinxed. There would be no shame in losing to a team flying high a division above, no post-mortem for a plucky defeat. Get back to that division; then think about the cup.

But Hibs have no intention of losing this game. This is what the local rivalry does to players, even if they know nothing of Duncan, Baker, Tommy Traynor and Willie Bauld, just some of the heroes of these frantic affairs. They hear the unholy racket made by the stands and think: this game matters. *A lot*. It's because Hibs have played well, presented a real threat to Hearts, that the home fans in this giant sardine tin are shouting so loudly, scarves twirling, to try and help the boys in maroon through the tie. And maybe, too, despite their ill-fortune and uselessness through history, it's what the cup does to Hibs.

Niklas Gunnarsson replaces Gray to revive Scandi associations with the Edinburgh derby. In the 1960s John Madsen was a steely centre-half for Hibs; Rene Moller and Roald Jensen clever forwards for Hearts. Jensen had a statue erected in his honour in the Norwegian city of Bergen but there's no evidence that Joe Baker ever collided with it.

Gunnarsson also peps up this Hibee challenge. Since his quiet debut in the previous round at Raith, he's got the measure of Scottish football, understands its blood and thunder better, also its thud and blunder. He helps Marvin Bartley assemble an oil-drum raft in the middle of the park from which the team can mount a comeback.

Heavy lifting is invariably required against Hearts; they like a tackle down Gorgie way. These Jambos have amassed the most red and yellow cards of any side in their league with opposition managers lining up to remark in awed and occasionally fearful tones about their brawn. In a competition which Hearts would love to win – and a six on the end of the year has often coincided with the desired outcome – it won't be enough to have only a couple of men tackling like demons; everyone has to do it.

In the past Hibs' creatives have not turned up against Hearts. Artistic types have gone all faint at the rumbustiousness of a derby while to others you would pose the urgent question from an old TV commercial: 'Mummy, why are your hands so soft?' McGinn and Henderson, though, are relishing this contest. They realise that time on the ball is going to be hard-won. The previous week in the League Cup semi McGinn had capped a vibrant performance with the winning goal and a call-up to the Scotland squad will now follow. That was also the first public performance of his song. To the tune of

Billy Ray Cyrus's prog-rock classic 'Achy Breaky Heart', it goes like this: 'We've got McGinn, super John McGinn/I just don't think you understand/He's Alan Stubbs' man, he's better than Zidane/We've got super John McGinn.'

For the Hibee generation who grew up watching Pat Stanton the two Alexes, Cropley and Edwards in the 1970s, there has been plenty of exasperation since. These guys were all desperate to keep moving forward; it was as if they had the same respiratory system as sharks and their lives depended on prodding the ball ahead of them, looking for interesting things to do with it. Not all of their successors have been quite so keen to advance. On especially gloomy days it seemed like Hibs were lining up with the old sand-dancing vaudeville act Wilson, Keppel and Betty strung out across the halfway line, edging along it and never advancing. Honorable exceptions were Russell Latapy, Franck Sauzee, Mickey Weir, Scott Brown and Kevin Thomson. Otherwise there have been too many fair-to-middling, middle-of-the-road, stuck-in-the-middle, mid-beige midfielders.

McGinn, though, is exceptional at belting straight at the heart of the opposition. His charges are barrelling and buccaneering, maybe not beautiful, and you might call his awkward, hunched gait Igor-like, but none of the assistants to fiendish villains in gothic melodramas who answered to that name could run 400m like this one. He's deceptively strong – 'a bull o' a boy' according to Kevin Thomson, a substitute today in his third spell at Hibs. Thomson used to be that bull but doubtless he's glad that McGinn does the tough running now.

The Zinadine-esque pirouette which inspired the chant is on show today as both McGinn and Henderson confirm that neither is a member of a Dishonorable Company of Midfielders Passing Sideways. Hibs are dominating the second half but until the eightieth minute it looks like this will be another hard-luck derby for them. Then McGinn lurches threateningly and feeds Henderson out right.

Henderson is quickly closed down, forcing him further wide, and there seems no prospect of the player being able to contrive anything meaningful – but he manages to squirt over a cross. Cropley did something similar against Rangers in the 1971 semi-final, creating a goal from an impossible position for Jimmy O'Rourke – and there's no higher praise than a comparison with the player nicknamed 'Sodjer' because he was born in the garrison town of Aldershot. Jason Cummings has a bit more to do than O'Rourke because of the delivery arriving slightly behind him. But with a twist of the neck he's able to arc the ball towards the far corner of the net. Possibly unable to believe its lazy parabola, there's a split-second delay before the Hibs fans behind the Hearts keeper Neil Alexander realise their team are right back in the tie.

Cummings is simply thrilled to score at Tynecastle, having been rejected by Hearts as a sixteen-year-old. This might make him seem like a player in need of validation – he isn't, not at all. Cummings is possibly the most cocksure young man in Scotland. In entertaining post-match interviews, he's revealed how his left foot can open tins of beans, how other goals have demonstrated 'the touch of an angel, ye ken?' If he was to get anywhere near a microphone today he'd probably make Cristiano Ronaldo seem shy and awkward. And this goal will have been especially satisfying with Stokes having arrived to a fanfare to provide the team with more goals and swagger. It's a little reminder that Cummings is the top scorer around these parts and pretty swaggersome himself.

The equaliser comes a minute into injury-time and owes much to the never-say-die of Hanlon and McGregor who've both delivered stirring performances in the back line. The latter is determined to be first to a McGinn corner but his thumping header is parried. Hanlon pounces on the rebound, belting his shot as he falls, and it's too hard and fast to be stopped by the thicket of legs in front of him.

Even then there's still time for Hibs to almost lose the tie when first Gunnarsson deflects a Hearts' effort onto his own bar and from the resultant corner Thomson has to head off the line. That would have been a prime example, I suppose, of the team Hibsing it. But haven't the Jambos, from being two-nil up, not just gone and Heartsed it? You'd struggle to argue that, I suppose, given Hibs' long-established tradition for playing the winsome graduate who falls out of her dress on the way to collecting her honours degree. But what a stormer of a game this has been.

The Hibs fans celebrate the draw like a victory with another blast of the McGinn song. In the bowels of the antiquated main stand the Proclaimers' 'Sunshine on Leith', the adopted Hibs anthem, drifts out of the away dressing-room and along the corridors where a commissionaire helps an old-timer into his snug overcoat. 'Aye,' says the veteran, possibly able to remember back sixty-one years to when the Terrible Trio walloped the Famous Five at this equally snug venue, 'the Hibs were good the day.'

But this is the Scottish Cup and even with home advantage in the replay nothing is certain for Hibs. Indeed it seems that if there is one certainty concerning the Hibees and the cup it's disappointment. In '71 Arthur Duncan's galloping goal was ultimately in vain as the team would lose that semi to Rangers. Eight years later Hibs would win the next cup derby – an encounter disrupted by a hooligan pagger on the pitch which could have been sponsored by Cowan Tailoring – and went all the way to the final only for Rangers, again, to shatter the dream. History repeats for Hibs, and Hibstory seems to mean they will always fail.

The next four capital encounters were won by Hearts. The victories in 1994, when the outplayed Jambos stole the tie at the death and 2009 with Hibs' Steven Fletcher being harshly sent off, had an element of fortune about them. Not so the others. These were the occasion of Zibi's Hampden howlers and the worst derby of them all.

NINE

'THAT WAS THE GAME WHERE EVERYTHING CHANGED . . .'

SO, 2-0 DOWN to Hearts at Tynecastle with ten minutes remaining, Alan Stubbs, and you still want the title and still believe you can win it – do you let the Scottish Cup go at that moment and prioritise the way many Jambo fans believe their club did to secure automatic promotion in 2015, focusing on the league?

'No,' he says, 'I wasn't prepared to kiss the cup goodbye – no way. I go into each and every game wanting to win it. I always have done and always will. We'd played well at Tynecastle and I just didn't believe that that one was going to finish up with us losing and going out of the cup.

'That was the game where everything changed. I think in years gone by Hibs would have eventually been beaten three-nil, maybe even four-nil. But that day they showed a new mindset. They absolutely refused to let Hearts win. It was pivotal.

'I thought we were the better team before they scored their goals. We had injuries but weren't going to feel sorry for ourselves and Niklas [Gunnarsson] and Thommo [Kevin Thomson] came on and played their parts in the fightback.

'We had a Premiership team, 2-0 up on their own ground, pinned back in their own half and we were relentless. Robbie [Neilson] tried to change his tactics but this had no effect. We were wave after wave. It seemed only a matter of time before we made the breakthrough.

'If I had to pick one player who I thought might have been able to score that first goal – and it really did take some contriving – it wouldn't have been Jason [Cummings]. I mean, he's opportunistic, no doubt about that, but with his head? He doesn't open tins of beans with his head; it's not his most potent attribute. When it comes to heading Jason is more concerned with how his hairstyle might be disrupted than with making contact with a flying football.'

Once Hibs got one back Stubbs was in no doubt they would find an equaliser even though they left it late. He was delighted that Paul Hanlon, another fan-turned-player for whom pulling on the green-and-white is special, was the man to send Hibbies into raptures, not least because he bears the emotional scars of losing so spectacularly in the all-Edinburgh cup final.

'When I came to the club Paul was a really comfortable footballer with good ability as a ball-playing centre-back but maybe he wasn't the most dominant in the position. We spoke about how, if he wasn't going to be able to muscle guys out of the way, he needed to be cleverer than they were. But he did get stronger. He grew in stature. He became a bigger man. Look at that goal he scored: who was ever going to beat him to the ball?'

TEN

THE HORROR! THE HORROR!

THE ONE AND only time I travelled to Hampden by a route other than the classic original it was my nadir as a fan and, beyond the deaths of my parents, I'm struggling to think of a worse day, ever.

'There it is again!'

'Where?'

'Right bloody there!'

Rab and I had just driven past Shettleston Bowling Club for a fourth time and a great friendship seemed about to unravel. A friendship founded on prog-rock, Tennent's Lager, the harsh, maverick, inspired teachings of Edinburgh's Broughton High School and the films – or if none were available then the hot-panted, wetlook-booted appearances in the *Daily Express*'s William Hickey column – of Susan George. And not forgetting Hibernian FC, the reason we were daundering around the east end of Glasgow on the morning of 19 May, 2012.

The classic original route to the national stadium, the one I'd always taken with my father, was staying on the M8 all the way to Glasgow's city centre then crossing over from there, but on this fateful day my chum and I had decided to follow the signs saying 'Football traffic'.

We were lost. Not long-beard-and-rags, crawling-through-the-desert lost but the befuddlement meant we couldn't stay calm, think straight or do anything other than keep chugging past this company of bowlers and their pebble-dashed headquarters. If only we'd read that sign in full:

Football traffic. That is, take this route if you've come to watch an authentic team. Be wary of loan signings, guys for whom your beloved club might be just another casual stopover. Such as: players selected with less than maximum scientific rigour from the utility-player mountain, almost as big as a butter mountain, or who're part of holding-midfielder landfill. Players hardened by the system not to fall in love with your club; that's their excuse, anyway. They won't kiss the badge – not a bad thing – but this lot may not actually be able to find the badge on the shirt. Of course, they may be brilliantly ruthless mercenaries, faces blackened to blend with the night, polonecks rolled high, Robert Shaw among them, all belayed together, who get the job done without emotion and depart without goodbyes. Best of luck, then, but if you're unsure, turn the car round and head for home.

A lot to try and cram onto a road sign? This was Hibs we were talking about. It was all necessary. We were on the wrong road, or not the one we knew; it would presumably get us to Hampden eventually, if we could just leave the bowling club behind. So why had we taken it? Maybe in the hope our cup luck would change. Or perhaps it was about safety in numbers. The day probably wasn't going to work out too well. In fact it was very likely to be hellish. Therefore best not to be alone.

Also, as well as wanting to be among our kin we were maybe seeking acceptance and approval from the wider football community. We thought 'Football traffic' could apply to Hibs like it did other clubs, bring us into the body of the kirk, make us feel we weren't any different from other fans who'd had a big Hampden day out, forgetting that most medium-to-big teams had won the Scottish Cup far more recently.

Inclusivity is a big thing now, isn't it? Every BBC drama features a character with a wooden leg and/or a glass eye. But when it comes to the cup, inclusivity isn't inclusive enough to include Hibs, and that was certainly true in 2012. We were NFI.

Looking back on that day, deconstructing it with the help of my therapist, I wonder if Rab and I might have deliberately tried to get lost. Maybe we were footering around in Shettleston because we couldn't face the dread-inevitable. That would have been entirely understandable. This Scottish Cup final – the twelfth for the club – was unique: one we were desperate to win but also a game we were terrified of losing. Playing Celtic or Rangers, opponents in our previous two finals, we obviously didn't want to lose, but once we'd got over the disappointment we accepted the outcomes. Further back in history, when Hibs lost finals to Clyde and Airdrie, I'm sure the defeats hurt but the fans – made of sterner stuff, of course – would have got over them. How were we supposed to recover from being beaten by Hearts?

This was to be the all-Edinburgh final, the biggest derby ever, the ultimate score-settler, the last word in who rooled, OK, capital-wise, the Auld Reekie Deathmatch. Lose it, and Hibbies would never again be allowed to mention the 7-0 annihilation of Hearts in 1973. Win, and we would have something even bigger to brag about. Toot our horns in built-up areas about. Clunkily, contrivedly mention at every possible opportunity. Re-set our pin numbers to commemorate.

0-7 6-2. The most famous Hibee victory over the Jambos, closely followed by the second-most-famous. Steal my bank card, phone and computer, key in those digits, and you'd have all of me. My money and my worldly goods – yes, including the King Crimson fortieth anniversary remasters. It would be difficult to hold onto my wife and kids if all I had left to my name was an unwanted doubler of the match programme from Hibs' unsuccessful 1965 defence of the Summer Cup, having sold the collection to vainly stay afloat.

Hibs fans would have been nervous about this game anyway, even if they hadn't just spent the season watching a team in which they didn't really believe stumble to eleventh in the Premier League. Any lower and they'd have been relegated.

They would have been nervous anyway because Hearts, even when not a great side playing brilliantly, can usually be relied upon to prevail in the derby. Hibs, we felt back then, needed to be a fantastic side playing out-of-this-world to win and in 2012 they weren't that for sure.

Hearts had a toughness that Hibs couldn't match, neither mentally nor physically. Hibs were 'soft-centred'; you heard this all the time. Hearts, using the sweetie analogy, were a sharp-edged, rock-hard chunk of toffee from Duncan's, the Edinburgh confectioners whose factory was near Logie Green, venue for the only other all-Embra cup final 116 years previously.

Was it any wonder, then, that Rab and I were cowering and snivelling in Shettleston? We'd shown some initiative by wandering over to the bowling club and finding it full of Hibbies who'd booked it for a pies-all-round lunch. For a brief moment we thought about sitting in the car until they'd finished then following their bus to Hampden but decided that would be pathetic, even for Hibs fans, and send the wrong message to the team, if indeed they were paying attention.

The countdown to the final had been an entire week of superstitions and sucking up to the Almighty. If the next car passing me is green, if the next girl is blonde, if the next bus has a bald man on it, if I can remember all the Roxy Music B-sides – real childish nonsense – then Hibs will win the cup. Please God please, I'll be a model citizen for the rest of my life if you can just arrange for us to beat Hearts . . .

Jambo pals were doing exactly the same. A build-up of jitteriness and fretting. Lucky socks, lucky pants, lucky string vests, lucky stringback driving gloves, lucky RainMates, lucky balaclavas, lucky car air-fresheners recreating the Gorgie breweries' stink. Every exiled fan was returning for this one. Every ex-player was offering his tuppenceworth, some for the first time since decimalisation. Tickets were changing hands for thousands of pounds.

Rab and I eventually stopping prevaricating. We called up our friend Kevin who, like an air traffic controller, guided us by phone all the way to Mount Florida and our pre-match trattoria. A Celtic fan, Kevin had organised our tickets. He knew other Celtic supporters with Hampden debentures, the football equivalent of a property timeshare, fixed for late spring. Their club are almost always in the final but weren't that year, Hearts defeating them in the semi with a last-minute penalty.

Debentures, antipasti. How the make-up of Scottish football fan has changed from the days when he was more about dentures and Auntie Jean's mince. The lunch was excellent, a convivial gathering of fellow sufferers and hopeless cases including Simon, whose Auntie Phyllis' cautionary words had been adopted by our group as a gloomy motto: 'Remember, the Hibs will always let you down.'

We recalled the old Hibees managers who sanctioned boring football – 'If it's entertainment you want, go to the cinema,' grumped one – which often persuaded us to order another bottle of wine and miss the game. But we couldn't do that, tempting as it was. A little voice – admittedly down to the level of a gnat's whisper – was telling us that in football you never really knew what was going to happen. And imagine if Hibs won the cup and you chumps missed it?

We were pretty sure we knew what was going to happen – we'd seen Pat Fenlon's team play. 'I looked in his eyes and saw a winner,' declared the chairman when Fenlon was the surprise appointment six months previously, only for him to quickly rack up fourteen league defeats. Somehow, his side battled through to the final.

I repeat: your team is your team and in Hibs' case, your valley of death is your valley of death. You can't hide. Yes, we'd seen how this movie usually ended. We'd certainly seen how *Just a Boys' Game* ended – many times. Peter McDougall's brilliant *Play for Today*, about a 1970s gangland Greenock power-struggle, had the semi-retired top droog tell pals trying to dodge the final confrontation: 'Yez don't go back.' We were no tough guys, far from it, but we had to take what was coming our way.

Mount Florida is such a pleasant place in which to witness a minor tragedy: sturdy villas, trim gardens, roses and chrysanthemums abounding. We got to our seats just in time for kick-off and Hampden at that moment looked fantastic. The invasion by the Edinburgh brigades, one green the other maroon, had been a highly successful military operation and it was possible to briefly put aside our fear and feel some civic pride. Everyone seemed to be there; no one was stuck at Shettleston. Also at that moment the stadium was at its loudest. This had been the largest gathering for these old foes since the 1950s when, don't forget, men wore ties and had a finely-developed sense of restraint. The anticipation for what was a genuine event, rare in Scottish football, almost blew the roof off. The cacophony was like Wagner had joined Slade for the afternoon. But one lot were going to be devastated, possibly suicidal, by the end.

*

That would be us. Hibs took the field in shirts better suited to the beach and let Hearts kick sand in their faces for the entire ninety minutes. Not just out-muscled, though, Fenlon's team were outwitted. The manager had watched the Jambos' Ian Black dominate two derby victories in the league but seemed to have no plan for curbing his playmaker threat. This was a fellow who, by his own admission, invited half a dozen clatterings from opponents every game, but in that final didn't receive one. The Hearts manager, Paulo Sergio, who had demonstrated that when his side were struggling he could effect the transformations required to win games, was simply too smart for Fenlon whose wizard wheeze of shipping in half a team of temporary signings proved to be disastrous. The players barely looked like they knew each other. Worse, they seemed doltishly unaware of the death-or-glory nature of a cup final derby and how the fans of the losing team would be haunted by the defeat, probably for evermore.

Chaotically and without a thought to damage-limitation, Hibs allowed Rudi Skacel, another dangerous player with previous in the fixture, to roam free and net a fifth goal when there was still a quarter of an hour remaining. I know we said a Hearts victory would render the events of 1 January, 1973 irrelevant, but Rab and I were among those sneaking out of Hampden who were desperately hoping the Jambos wouldn't get to seven. That victory was all we had, but really, we had nothing left.

Hibernian 1 Hearts 5. Who's ever been thrashed like that in a Scottish Cup final? Well, Hibs, actually – beaten 6-1 by Celtic in 1972. Hearts had a better team and a better manager and had been expected to win a game suddenly upgraded from the biggest-ever derby to the biggest game, full stop, in the history of both clubs. But the manner in which Hibs capitulated was a shattering blow for those fans racing back to Edinburgh to take the phone off the hook and shut the curtains.

Rab and I went home the traditional route. We'd taken the wrong road to watch our team embarrass themselves epicly in the wrong competition. Hibs were never going to win the Scottish Cup; you'd be insane to think otherwise. A summer of humiliation lasting, oh, the rest of our lives seemed to lie ahead. D-list celebrities, politicians and visiting dignitaries were photographed making a five-finger, one-finger gesture having apparently been persuaded that this was a customary Edinburgh greeting and display of friendliness. Those with Hibs connections found themselves duped into offering the same sign, proof that the Hibees' cock-up was ongoing and unstoppable.

I'm old enough to know better, to have other interests, to have a family to look after and worry about, but this was an absolutely crushing moment. Meanwhile the loan players left the club. Minimal info about their involvement in a cup final might have looked good on the CV; actual footage probably wouldn't have enhanced the showreel too much.

Name that team? The Hibs line-up isn't burned in cherishable memory. Indeed in 2012 Hibbies fully expected to be challenged to list it in a never-changing pub quiz in Hell, when they eventually went to that place, their cup-less days on Earth mercifully over.

*

'It will haunt me for ever, that final,' says Garry O'Connor. 'A terrible, terrible day.'

We're talking in a cafe in North Berwick where the striker has found maturity, peace and happiness after a chaotic career of big-money moves, misadventures in Moscow, Barnsley and Siberia, drugs busts, pensioners' grass-cutting as penance – and lots of ruthless goals. It seems cruel to bring up the 5-1 hammering but O'Connor reckons demons have to be confronted and he's well used to doing that.

'The whole thing was a complete fiasco,' he says. 'None of the team knew what they were supposed to be doing. I had a little injury in the lead-up; there were five or six of us like that. As a result Pat Fenlon couldn't shape the team. Then, just when we thought we knew what the line-up was going to be, he changed Sparky's [Leigh Griffiths] role and brought in the Honduran [Jorge Claros]. That rocked the boat.'

O'Connor was back at Hibs for a second spell. He scored the winner in the Russian Cup final, but a promising Scottish Cup run in his first stint at Easter Road, netting in every round including a handsome 3-0 win against Rangers at Ibrox, came to an abrupt end when he was sold to Lokomotiv Moscow. His first time at the club there had been a terrific *esprit de corps*. Some of the friendships went all the way back to juvenile football. This was a mainly Scottish team which played together, socialised together and would frequently bump into each other at the Toni + Guy hair salons in Edinburgh which offered free cuts to the cocky, talented young sportsmen-about-town who'd be great advertising for their crimping. The second time there just wasn't the same camaraderie.

'The loan signings started arrived in January. There were maybe fourteen of them – it was crazy. I remember saying to my close friends, Stacky [Graham Stack], Sprouler [Ivan Sproule] and Ian [Murray]: 'What's going on here?' It had been a pretty awful season battling relegation and the cup final turned out to be a horrible end to it. In the dressing-room after the final whistle some of the new guys were laughing away. There was an atmosphere. The result had really hurt the boys who cared. So there was a fight . . .'

Seconds after being presented with his runners-up medal O'Connor tossed it away. He was then on the move again, having had an offer from Tom Tomsk FC, but heading to Siberia after that result seemed the right thing to do. 'It sounds like the jail, doesn't it?' he laughs gloomily. Some of his team-mates needed locking up after their performances at Hampden. Many of the fans who suffered would have willingly submitted to incarceration in a far-off land in the hope they'd be able to forget all about that delusional day when they thought they could beat their old, old rivals and win the cup.

ELEVEN

'DEMONIC ELECTRONIC SUPERSONIC MO-MO-MOMENTUM'

16 February 2016
Hibernian 1 Hearts 0

I'M TRYING TO remember the last time I queued for tickets. It might have been Deep Purple at the Odeon, Yes at the Empire or Pink Floyd at the Usher Hall. It was definitely music and not football, though.

I didn't have to be a devout fan of the bands I witnessed 'In concert', as the tickets would have it. As long as one of my school-friends was, that was enough. The rest of us always got something out of the evening, such as gawping at willowy girls in afghan coats, speculating about how long it took the willowy girls' boyfriends to grow a Zapata moustache, or a Zappa one, and studying the roadies' lengthy set-up routine. The latter was probably boring for everyone else, but it fascinated four berks in loon-pants determined to squeeze maximum joy from the 80p gig-going experience.

We also loved the camaraderie of the queue. The sale of tickets would happen some months before the show, and after this was announced fairly cryptically, buying them would require an early start, possibly sharing the first bus of the morning with coal miners (that's social history right there), fried-egg rolls and tea in polystyrene cups for pavement sustenance – and a good excuse for the teachers for lessons missed. We felt brave, we felt exotic, and the sniggering junior longhairs delighted in telling bemused OAPs passing the queue that while they might well have enjoyed bingo nights at the selfsame venue, the world was changing fast.

This was all pre-online booking, which is the way of the ticketing world now, so I'm not sure why I'm in a queue at Easter Road when I could be being made to wait on the phone for tickets for the Hearts replay, then charged a fee for the inconvenience. It feels very 1970s to be doing this, always a pleasant sensation, and maybe Hibs will deliver a 1970s performance against the Jambos, those usually ending in thrilling victory.

Perhaps everyone else here is similarly optimistic but the tie is not close to being won because it's now shifted to Leith. Hearts will surely still be Hearts and there must be a good chance that for Hibs the Scottish Cup will still be the Scottish Cup. Viz, a competition we're not supposed to win. Nevertheless, the game will be a sell-out. Unusually it won't be shown live on TV so if you want to see it you'll have to be there. This match just gets more and more retro. Any minute now I'm thinking I'll be joined in the line by a lad in mauve bell-bottoms with curtained hair and carrying a Jethro Tull LP. This doesn't quite happen, the album being brandished is in fact one by Van Der Graaf Generator (joke). But we get chatting, this fellow and I, about Hibs' prospects and what will come to be known as 'The Anthony Stokes Conundrum'.

Stokesy is firmly in the tradition of wayward Hibs strikers. Brilliant, infuriating, don't-know-what-they've-got. Rascals, ravers, radges. Big on innate, dead-eyed talent, short on application. Gallus, greedy, great on their day. Front-page headlines as well as back-page ones. Infuriating for their managers but impossible to leave out of the team. Derek Riordan was one, and Garry O'Connor, and Leigh Griffiths.

And here's another hugely improbable, completely ridiculous connection between two of them, suggesting that Elvis Presley doesn't figure on the mixtape the Easter Road bad boys might pass round each other. In 2004, O'Connor was accused of assaulting an Elvis impersonator. In 2013, just a fortnight after doing down Hibs in the Scottish Cup final for Celtic, Stokes was accused of assaulting an Elvis impersonator. In January Stokes' trial was postponed until the end of the year after the Dublin court was told he'd 'started a new job'. Playing for Hibs, trying to win them the ever-elusive cup. 'Good luck with that,' might have been the magistrate's comment.

O'Connor and Riordan were exact contemporaries, scored a million goals for their boys' club, and flourished at Easter Road under Tony Mowbray, a football version of Lord Shaftsbury. While the latter was a social reformer who saved lads from having to clean chimneys, Mowbray pointed a youthful team towards the sunlight after the dour football of his predecessor, Bobby Williamson. The players chose flamboyant haircuts to match their new style of play and unsurprisingly the frontmen ensured theirs were the zazziest. O'Connor was the first to move, becoming British football's first export to Russia, and scored the winning goal in a cup final for which he was presented with a flash car. Gaz and Ferraris were a dangerous combo; he wrote one off costing £100,000. Unfortunately the stats which defined what should have been his peak years were more about squandered earnings than goals. He blew £4 million on cars, cocaine and champagne and even splashed £2,000 on a tracksuit.

Riordan once threatened to become the Scottish top-flight's all-time highest goalscorer but also made bad career choices, rotting on the bench at Celtic. Deek ventured to China where the food was an issue: 'There was chicken feet, what I was told was frog and other no' right stuff,' he once told me. Recreationally, Riordan also got into bother and was banned from every nightclub in Edinburgh. Both he and O'Connor wandered back to Easter Road, that diamond sharpness gone from their play, and were only able to offer occasional reminders of their casual, cocky brilliance. Lost boys, the pair of them.

Griffiths – Sparky – used to cheer on these two as a Hibs fan and during an action-packed two seasons at Easter Road scored the winning goals in consecutive Scottish Cup semi-finals and also reportedly headbutted his manager and punched the assistant manager. He moved on to Celtic where off-field malarkey continued to be an issue, but then he settled down and was voted Scotland's Player of the Year, seeming to have learned from the mistakes of others.

Griffiths couldn't win the cup and nor could O'Connor or Riordan, the latter's most promising moment coming when he fired Hibs ahead in a semi-final which would be lost at the death, so what about Stokes? 'He just needs to get fit,' reckons the lad behind me in the queue, 'and pass more. Although saying that you can see his cleverness, always looking for little nooks and crannies where he can cause the most damage and trying shots no one expects.'

Of most immediate concern is whether we're going to obtain tickets as we're still a good half mile from the sales windows. Frank Dougan, the fans' rep on the Hibs board, has already been right along the line, counting the queue's needs, saying it will be touch and go for us. Another hour passes during which we recall goals scored by our scallywag strikers against Hearts at Easter Road. There was a Stokes equaliser in a New Year game, an O'Connor last-minute winner for ten-man Hibs and one Riordan screamer with the right foot and another with the left, the latter prompting Scottish football's great ginger-owl commentator-oracle Archie Macpherson to hyperventilate: 'That's an exocet!' But as a note of caution for Hibs fans, and it's traditional we have these, Griffiths never scored against the Jambos here. An outrageous, long-distance free-kick walloped the underside of the crossbar and bounced a good two feet over the line but was ruled out. The greatest lost goal by a lost boy, ever.

Finally we reach the front of the queue. Amazingly, I get the last two tickets, which would probably be seized upon as a highly promising cup omen if I supported any other club. I turn round to sympathise with my new-found friend but he's already trudging away from the ground. What's worse is that I've almost certainly only imagined him having a 1970s record collection back at home. I don't think he's going to be able to console himself with Groundhogs, Spooky Tooth and Bloodwyn Pig.

*

While Tynecastle is claustrophobic, Easter Road is panoramic. From the top rows you can see mountains and oceans. Okay, you can see Arthur's Seat, the impotent volcano where my Auntie Nan, a spinster, encountered a flasher, and the Firth of Forth where the super-yachts of the English Premier League's oligarchs are noticeable by their absence and instead we get to watch dredgers and sewage-dumpers. Okay, we can't really see much in the way of vista since the new stands went up, but hopefully you get my drift: Easter Road is different and tonight it feels special.

There's no TV because leading oligarch Roman Abramovich's Chelsea are playing Paris Saint-Germain, another obscenely rich mob, in the Champions League and this tournament demands that nothing can possibly divert attention from the opulent fare. It's a nice thought, isn't it? The world's wealthiest clubs running scared of Jason Cummings, socks round his ankles, strutting, flicking his hair, flashing that Krispy Kreme grin.

To get round the telly ban, some chancer-media entrepreneurs have tonight introduced Periscoping to Scottish football. They point their smartphones at the pitch, relaying the action to the folks back home via Twitter. Shaky visuals and semi-drunken noises-off are supposed to add to the experience and you just wonder what coverage of the fourth minute is like. This is when Hibs take the lead with who else but Cummings the scorer.

While Hearts enjoyed a break thanks to the bad weather, Hibs had played a gruelling league game on a slushy pitch just three nights before. But there is no sign of weariness in their electrifying start, urged on by a baying crowd on a chilly night. John McGinn sets off on a swashbuckling diagonal run, hurdling challenges, and springs David Gray racing up the right who, at the second attempt, crosses low for Cummings to pop the ball into the roof of the net. The player's celebration, directed at the fans of the club who didn't rate him as a kid, could be interpreted thus: 'Not bad, eh, you complete and utter spangles.'

The action is breathless, with Hearts denied an equaliser by an offside flag although before then Cummings really should have increased Hibs' advantage after being set up by Liam Henderson, rampaging all over the park as usual. Henderson joined Hibs at the same time as McGinn and was just as quick to endear himself to the fans. He has a song, too. It reworks Simon & Garfunkel's 'Mrs Robinson' – 'And here's to you Liam Henderson/The Hibees love you more than you will know' – and is the fans' plea to him to sign up to Easter Road permanently.

Tall, shaggy-haired, bold on the ball, he has passion to burn. Often he'll turn and roar his delight at something which has excited him. This can be a goal or simply the match having kicked off. He's an electricity sub-station on legs, sending a surge of volts round the team and the crowd, invigorating everyone on grey days. Hibs have had their share of guys who've played to the gallery, sliding across the turf in front of the noisiest and – they think – easiest-pleased stand when the ball is already on its way out of play. Henderson is not one of them. Nor is he one of those loanees who sulks and sees out the deal with the minimum of effort. Aged eighteen, he was sent out to Rosenborg and helped them achieve a Norwegian league and cup double and now he's giving everything to this cause, however temporary may be his stay.

Henderson is playing his part in a pulsating tie and in one sense it's a pity the game isn't being beamed into the nation's parlours. In another sense, though, the game is like the new Roxy Music LP when only Co-op shelf-stacking at weekends would secure me a copy. The game is more cherishable because it's not on TV and I'd had to get up early to obtain tickets. Thus I'm studying aspects of play more intently than usual, and trying to commit them to memory like the detail on that record's gateway sleeve ('Demonic electronic supersonic mo-mo-momentum . . . Clothes, make-up – Anthony Price, Kari-Ann's hair – Smile . . . Leaves of gold crossing thresholds & hearts').

Maybe for Scottish Cup supersonic mo-mo-momentum this game is going to rival Hibs' 4-3 win over Celtic in 1986, another tie blacked out by TV which now only exists in hugely embroided memory. But – and there's always a but with this club – for every encouragement the cup offers, history can propel us into the sidings after a crashing tackle.

This is a replay and I've seen Hibs lose twelve of them in the competition. Offered second chances to dispose of East Fife and Stirling Albion, they cocked up. Same with Arbroath in 1977 when a big away support lorded it around the Angus town, laughing at the tickets advertising a 'Grand football match'. But this was the home of the 36-0 world record-holders, proper cup history. On a blustery afternoon by the North Sea Hibs were fortunate they weren't hot-smoked like the local haddock. They took the Red Lichties back to Easter Road – and lost.

The 1970s were an especially bad decade for second-time defeats, seven in all. A last-minute leveller at Motherwell raised hopes; Hibbies greeted it by running screaming from Fir Park as if they were fleeing a burning building. That tie needed two replays before Willie Pettigrew, wild-haired with a ruthless striker's aim and a player Hibs had as a youngster then let go, settled it.

I also witnessed Hibs losing a replay at Dundee, 3-0 in 1974 when Eddie Turnbull's team were hotly tipped for the cup. Although that defeat, at a boisterous Dens Park with more than 30,000 squeezed inside, would have been another crushing blow, I cannot look back on the match with anything other than fondness because it was one of those rare occasions when I went to the football with my mother.

I followed Hibs all over Scotland with my father who, as a BBC Scotland producer, seemed to arrange his work round the fixture-list, apart from on two occasions. The first was at Falkirk's Brockville, an incredible five-goal thriller with differing fortunes for its veteran strikers, Joe Baker scoring the winner with a diving header but Alex Ferguson butting Hibs captain Pat Stanton and being sent off. In schoolboy parlance this was called 'panelling'. There was a week-long playground craze with many casualties reporting to the nurse with sore noses. It was astonishing to see an adult carry out some panelling, never mind a future knight of the realm.

That Dens replay fell on a school night, which under Dad's rule would have meant me missing it. A conspiratorial softer touch, Mum said: 'I won't tell if you won't.' So we took the road and the miles to Dundee together for the secret cup defeat in a highly conspicuous litany.

*

Now I'm passing the baton. My nine-year-old son is with me at Easter Road – only because it's half-term, I'm tough like my father – and he's singing the song about McGinn being better than Zidane every time his favourite player starts an attack, though I must admit I hesitated about introducing him to football.

Until his first game his life had consisted of absolute certainties. They tuck you up, your mum and dad. You don't have to eat the peas. Jump and you will be caught, cry and you will be cuddled. Everything Playmobil interlocks. Everything Pixar has a happy ending. But football doesn't quite work like that.

Disappointment is a given. Your team will rarely win anything. You'll sit on plastic seat in a breeze-block arena right through the coldest months. You'll see chancers, mercenaries, honest toilers, over-tattooed fools and poor role-models. And if your team are Hibs, you shouldn't get too excited about the Scottish Cup.

But this breeze-block arena is home. These Hibees, as presently constituted, are players to admire and, given a fair wind, be excited by. This is a heady performance with the only disappointment being that the lead is not greater come half-time. And it's too late, anyway: Archie is obsessed with Hibs.

We're in the West Stand, which was the old Main Stand, at the bottom end of the pitch when it had the slope. Currently learning about statistical probability at school, the boy wants to know how, on the toss of a coin, 50-50, Hibs invariably got to shoot down the hill in the second half of games. He wants to know about the half-time scoreboard, long since gone (Me: 'It was a slow, cumbersome procedure. The scoreboard operator had to walk round the pitch, climb the ladder, open the hatch, then once inside we watched his shadowed silhouette take the big letters and numbers from his hessian bag and hook them onto the board for us to check against the match programme.' Him: 'I dunno, Dad, it sounds quite exciting.'). He wants to know about the jazzy-American 'Goal!'-flashing electronic apparatus (first-generation, that was definitely rubbish, always going *phut*). He wants to know if the old high terracing really burst through the sky. He wants me to tell him again how, as Pat Stanton told me, you could stand at the top of the terracing and look back at the great mass of people streaming towards the ground, stretching beyond Lochend Pond and as far as the eye could see, all of them desperate to say they were there the night Hibs took on the mighty Real Madrid (and beat them). He wants me to tell him again how the mighty Barcelona kicked at the referee's door in their rage after Hibs had vanquished them, the holes being left for years as a memento of another unforgettable European night. Because all children love mildly scary stories, he wants me to tell him again how my father would plonk me at the wall at the bottom of the big terracing and stand twelve steps back, directly behind me, and how I'd keep looking around for him, only the swell and surge of all that hodden-grey humanity would push us further and further apart.

I get so many questions, every single game. And he already knows where he wants to be buried – in the graveyard behind the Famous Five Stand.

He can't believe that Willie Hamilton, grand illusionist for the Real victory, didn't play like that every week and generally squandered his talents. He can't believe that George Best, the same Bestie who I've shown him on YouTube destroying Scotland from the Northern Ireland wing, was briefly another of Hibs' errant geniuses and so asks me to tell him again how I met the man at the official opening of a Restalrig exhaust-fitting outlet a couple of hours before he'd make a fool out of the Celtic defence (though I leave out the bit about his eyes being bloodshot and his breath reeking of booze). He doesn't just want to know about the good Hibs players, but the bad and the terrible ones, too. I can tell he's not very impressed by my tale about Joe Baker coming back to the club in white boots and Easter Road throbbing with anticipation because, well, anything other than black footwear is the norm now, but he listens to humour me. And when I tell him at the break in this hectic game that Cummings is the first Hibee to score in four consecutive matches against Hearts since the great Alex Cropley, he says: 'When did he play? Oh, don't tell me: the 1970s.'

When Cropley was dictating a game's tempo the pitch had a gradient and the stadium had character, though we didn't know that's what you called the rusting corrugated iron painted emerald green on the sides of the Main Stand or the brutalist Cowshed at the north end where Clockwork Orange-inspired bovver boys would heartily recommend to any junior WPCs patrolling the perimeter: 'Get it up you while you're young!'

Now that it's McGinn who's doing the dictating, aided and abetted by Henderson, the ground has lost some of its individuality through homogeneous, non-quirky design, although you could say that about so many of them.

But Easter Road doesn't feel samey tonight. Not with it the most jam-packed any of us has ever seen the place. Not with the sense that this is a unique event. Not with this thrusting midfield play, always looking to be progressive, like rock music used to be. It's a close-run thing, but forced to choose between the tie and Pink Floyd at the Usher Hall I'd probably opt for the football.

In the second half Hearts attempt a comeback and have the ball in the net again but once more it's disallowed. The heroics are now being found in defence where Paul Hanlon alongside Darren McGregor, David Gray and Lewis Stevenson is immense. Like Stevenson, Hanlon has played in losing cup finals and various Hibee horror shows. Like Stevenson, he keeps coming back for more. And he's giving the very distinct impression he's fed up with this dismal run in the cup and wants it to end as soon as possible.

This tie isn't quite over yet and goalkeeper Mark Oxley sends agitation round the home stands with his time-wasting and gets himself booked. McGinn attempts a volley when the ball drops like a stone towards him. Alex Cropley, taking on a shot just like this, scored the fourth in the 7-0 match then famously, after what Hibbies call 'the greatest game in history', popped to his granny's for tea. McGinn's effort whizzes the wrong side of a post. But Super John has been irresistible tonight. As the man from the *Daily Mail* will put it, his supposed marker, Miguel Pallardo, had covered the entire park: 'He was everywhere the Hibs man had just been.'

In the crazy finale Hearts have Blazej Augustyn sent off and then Cummings, booked for his goal celebration, boots the ball away and he's off, too. But Hibs hold onto their advantage and the stadium erupts. Their best performance in a replay? Well, they've won some before, and overcoming Rangers in the 1972 semi-final they were exceptional, Stanton and his genius midfield accomplice Alex Edwards scoring the goals. The Rangers fans reckoned that to be a significant victory and marked it by tanning the Hibee supporters' bus windows. But this one gets pretty close.

The Edinburgh teams are linked through song: 'Hearts, Hearts, Glorious Hearts' and 'Glory, Glory to the Hibees' were both recorded by the old Scottish entertainer Hector Nicol and it's these versions which play before home matches at the respective grounds. Doubtless Jambos will claim their ditty as being the A-side. The songs' quaint references to 'Auld Reekie' and 'the continentals' make you smile.

But Hibs' post-match song, played at the final whistle of a famous victory, has rung round the world. Maybe it's very Hibs to have your anthem begin, 'My heart is broken . . .' and suffice to say there haven't been many public renditions because for this club heartbreak usually results.

'Sunshine on Leith' by the Hibee-supporting Proclaimers is a beautiful, sad, uplifting hymn which has resonated with fans thirled to the fact that winning isn't everything. Not expressly written as a football song, it's been pounced on by supporters for very obvious reasons: there's deeper meaning about life, love and loss in its verses but if all you want to do is roar the title when you're half-cut and teary, that's fine. Easy interpretations of the words stress the importance of community, family, loyalty, endeavour, being there, going back the next week – and the song makes a few thousand blind-love Hibbies thank dear departed fathers for saddling them for keeps with this great, stressful, exhausting and probably life-shortening commitment to a football team who play in Leith and are always hopeful of fair weather ahead.

Renditions of 'Sunshine on Leith' like the one after the 2007 League Cup triumph are heavily replayed on YouTube and have had fans of Nottingham Forest, Schalke 04, Newell's Old Boys of Argentina and various American gridiron outfits queueing up to acclaim it as the best football song ever. There's another spine-tingling performance tonight as the players do a lap of honour, hugging each other, waving to the fans and getting the love right back.

Again, the footage goes viral. They rave about the song at Inter Milan, Feyenoord, Borussia Monchengladbach. Over his fish fingers the following night, Archie replays it on the iPad eight times. I tell him that's his screen-time up and he looks at me as if to say: 'It's not my fault, Dad – you turned me into this monster.'

TWELVE

'I LOVE "SUNSHINE ON LEITH". I JUST WASN'T HEARING IT ENOUGH . . .'

THE SCOTTISH CUP is not yet a concept for Hibs. No footballer talks about winning the thing when it's only the fifth round, least of all Hibees. Fans are allowed to dream of course but the club's supporters have learned from bitter experience not to get carried away. When it comes to cup woe and dashed hopes, they've have been there, done that, bought the ball-and-chain.

And anyway, dashing your old rivals' hopes is its own concept. 'No one was talking about the cup,' Alan Stubbs says of his team after the draw at Tynecastle and leading up to the replay. 'It was all about Hearts, how we hadn't wanted to lose the first game and how we knew we had a great chance at Easter Road.'

Once again he's unsure of the score. 'Was it one-nil?' I tell him there are people who carry this vital info around with them; it's inked on their left calves along with the rest of the cup run. 'Well, I remember how good we were that night. We started brightly, scored right away and for the first quarter Hearts couldn't live with us.

'After that the Hibs fans were maybe thinking, the way derbies had gone in the past, that Hearts would get a goal but I never felt they would. Hearts had the upper hand in the fixture before I joined. They'd wormed into the heads of the Hibs supporters and I wanted them out. Before, Hearts believed they were going to win derbies; Hibs only hoped they would. But I think that changed over the two years I was there.

'Look at our record: only one defeat and we were unlucky that some of the draws weren't more wins for us. We'd be the better team in those matches and they'd need a fantastic strike to get them back into the game. And I've got to be honest: Robbie [Neilson] has done a really good job, but as a club Hearts didn't like that the tide was turning in our favour.'

Another thing burned in his memory: the fans singing 'Sunshine on Leith' at the final whistle. 'It's one of the most emotional football songs you will ever hear, anywhere in the world, and remembering it that night is making my spine tingle right now. I loved "Sunshine on Leith" from the first time I heard it but in the context of us giving the supporters big wins I just wasn't hearing it enough.'

Stubbs wanted a couple more roof-raising renditions before the season was done. Not that anyone was yet talking about Hibs winning the cup . . .

THIRTEEN

'THERE WAS SOMETHING ALMOST MOVING IN THEIR NOBLE FAILURE'

11 April, 1914 Celtic 0 Hibernian 0
16 April, 1914 (replay) Celtic 4 Hibernian 1

HIBS DIDN'T HIBS it in 1914. They simply failed to exploit, or forgot to pack, their 'strange, intangible yet so thoroughly potent something'.

This is what the *Edinburgh Evening Dispatch* said were the team's gifts in the build-up to the 1914 final. It's a fine piece of description, don't you think? One which, for fans who came along later in the club's interminable struggle, could easily attach to the sides they watched. Apart from the potency bit, perhaps.

Hibs were back in the final for the first time since winning the cup twelve years before. They were still managed by Dan McMichael, the hero of 1902, and the team were an interesting bunch.

There was Willie Allan, the goalkeeper: a native of Falkirk, cashier at the Carron Ironworks and therefore of a 'natural saving disposition,' the *Dispatch* suggested in its pen-portraits. The custodian was also a singer with 'a weakness for operatics' though he promised there would be 'no theatrics on the field of play'.

Captain Matta Paterson, the best billiard player in the side, was 'keen as mustard' with 'the energy of half a dozen men'. This was probably just as well, given Neil Girdwood was 'a middling golfer with a tendency to slice on the football pitch' while Alexander Grosart was 'neither bonnie nor orthodox'. Peter Kerr was 'one of the solidest plodding halves in the country', which sounds like a compliment (just).

Hibs' opponents were Celtic, same as in 1902, and the final was played at Ibrox. Hampden had been the venue but lost the right for a few years following an Old Firm riot, the sort of behaviour which is simply unacceptable on cup final day.

The 'Parkheaders' had the best of the game but Allan kept the safe locked. Maybe the goalie could after all have burst into Gilbert and Sullivan because Celtic's Ebenezer Owers, who sounded like he belonged in a jaunty ditty, had a hapless afternoon. The match, in front of a crowd of 60,000, finished goalless but Hibs might have nicked it. Chicago-born Robert Wilson, 'frail and shy to the verge of timidity', could have scored. Diminutive, dapper Willie Smith, a man with a 'pretty full bag of tricks', should have done. The replay was five days later, again at Ibrox. Celtic replaced Owers with Jimmy McColl – a masterstroke, for the young man grabbed two goals in the first ten minutes. Hibs played a 'good, stuffy club game' according to *The Scotsman,* but were simply outclassed. The *Edinburgh Evening News* stated that their defence was 'wonderfully, easily penetrated'. Celtic scored two more before Smith's consolation.

The second match, watched by 40,000, had been a 'fine evening outdoors,' according to the *Evening News,* just as long as you weren't among the 'Edinburgh Excursionists'. Defeat didn't cause the club and its supporters trauma, though – it was too early in the saga for that, and of course no one knew this was going to turn into a saga. Four final appearances in thirty-nine years' existence and two triumphs was about average. But maybe some trends were established.

Optimism in the build-up, expectancy – sound familiar? Then, come the big day, nerves puncture the mood. The occasion gets to the players. A cup malaise is suspected, but proves difficult to hold in a test-tube for detailed examination in the lab. Hibs would show 'pluck' in 1914 – a word set to figure in reports of the next four final defeats – but each time they deserved to lose.

There was certainly no self-indulgent ruminating on this setback. Three months later the world would be at war and the cup wouldn't be contested for another six years.

31 March, 1923

Celtic 1, Hibernian 0

Maybe there were more themes to the Hibs tale, not yet an epic, such as larger-than-life goalkeepers. The 1914 goalie, Willie Allan, was accorded the title 'His Magnificence'. But surely Allan had to bow down to Willie Harper of the 1923 team with his comic book-hero back-story.

Harper had been a blacksmith. He'd served on the Western Front with the Scots Guards with whom he was heavyweight boxing champ and an outstanding rugby player. Centre-forwards could barge keepers into the net in those days; they must have thought twice when confronted by this man-mountain. He was Scotland's goalie, too, never losing to England in four internationals, and would fetch a world-record £4,000 fee for a keeper when he moved to Arsenal. And that year, all the way to the final, he had a proud record of not conceding a goal.

Who was going to score to win the cup for Hibs? Maybe Ian McColl now that Celtic's secret weapon from 1914 had swapped sides. McColl was a speedster but he suffered injury problems and Celtic allowed him to leave, although perhaps they were about regret this. He'd proved just as prolific at Hibs and justified holding onto the appellation, 'The Sniper'.

The managers were the brothers Malley – Alec at Hibs and Willie at Celtic. Alec declared: 'The great day is near at hand . . . all the players are sound and fit . . . I am convinced our half-back line is much stronger.' The *Evening Dispatch* put his comments to Willie who retorted: 'You cannot predict with any certainty where either team will be superior. For a number of years now the fancied side in the Scottish Cup final have gone under.' Maybe this wasn't a 'row' between the managers or an 'amazing flare-up' on a par with what Alan Stubbs and either Mark Warburton or Peter Houston could be persuaded to have on a slow-news Tuesday. The bosses were more restrained in those days and so were the press.

The *Evening Dispatch* tried to recall the final of nine years before, with understandable difficulty. 'Looking back over the dark days of war, and the almost equally dark days of a troubled peace, that event seems very distant now,' the paper admitted, 'but the passing of years has been very kind to many of those who were then engaged, and several reappear in the fight today.'

The paper, though, didn't want a sombre occasion; this was cup final day. Where, then, were the ricketties? Where were the flags? Banned from the stadium, apparently. There was no band either and all in all the build-up to kick-off was 'a trifle slack'. The match, in front of what *The Scotsman* called 'a grand gathering of 80,000', had better be good.

But Hibs, despite their positivity beforehand, didn't start 'chokeful of confidence'. Celtic's half-back line were a match for their much-hyped opposite numbers. Hibs' Harry Ritchie, expected to be 'the best wingman on view', was well shackled, as was Jimmy Dunn, a future Wembley Wizard in the Scotland team which thrashed England 5-1 in 1928. And Sniper McColl was firing blanks.

Celtic weren't brilliant either. There was sarcasm from the crowd over the number of times the ball was booted skywards and the threat this posed to aircraft, presumably a popular terracing gag of the immediate post-war years. With not much else to write about, the

Evening News padded out its report thus: 'The inspection of the goal nets was carried out by Mr Dougray and his assistants.'

But the Celts did just enough to win the game and their tenth cup, their score coming when Harper raced out to collect a through-ball only for Joe Cassidy to reach it first and head home. Some were reluctant to blame the great man but the *Evening News* headlined their report: 'Many a slip! Cup not yet for Edinburgh.'

19 April 1924
Airdrieonians 2 Hibernian 0

Undeterred, Willie Harper was back between the sticks for the following season's final – indeed they all were. An unchanged team and an unchanged outlook from Alec Malley. 'We are quietly confident of winning,' the manager asserted.

Hibs had beaten Airdrie in the league the week before but they would have been foolish to underestimate the Lanarkshire team, runners-up in the old First Division two years running, with an attack featuring a couple of Scottish football's bonniest young talents, Hughie Gallacher and Bob McPhail. This would be the Diamonds' brightest shining era.

The *Evening Dispatch* reported a tentative start from Hibs in the Ibrox final in front of a 60,000 crowd, which might have had something to do with them going a goal down in the first two minutes, Willie Russell the scorer. Airdrie were showing a 'fine breeziness' with Gallacher a constant danger and a second from Russell wasn't long in coming. Maybe there was an element of fortune about both goals, said the *Evening News*, but the best team won their first cup.

Hibs had an obsession. Not yet with the cup itself, they were determined to field the same eleven as the year before, to the extent of gambling on players' fitness. 'The team fell a trifle softy,' added the

Evening News. 'The men have had a heavy time and staleness may have imposed itself. They have been sailing under bare poles.'

After that, Hibs peered to where the sea meets the sky for a glint of the Scottish Cup but to no avail. They wouldn't reach another final for twenty-three years, the longest absence from the showpiece in their history.

19 April 1947
Aberdeen 2 Hibernian 1

Hibs had some abject cup defeats in the 1930s – same as every other decade, really. But they turned up in the semi-finals just before war shut down the competition again and when football resumed in 1946 they sought to tap into the national mood of renewed optimism and hope. A 9-1 thrashing of Queen of the South in the league opener was mirrored by an 8-0 thumping of Alloa Athletic in the first round of the cup. Gordon Smith, the greatest-ever Hibee, scored in both games while Jock Weir struck four each time. When it came to the cup-tie Smith had been joined by two more of the men who would form Scotland's most swashbuckling forward-line.

Gordon Smith, Bobby Johnstone, Lawrie Reilly, Eddie Turnbull, Willie Ormond. Smith! Johnstone! Reilly! Turnbull! Ormond! The names of the Famous Five are shouted during the crackly 78rpm recording of 'Glory, Glory to the Hibees' which has fanfared every game at Easter Road since the immortals hung up their clumpy Cotton Oxfords. All of their cup-questing heirs, some in horribly 'modernised' shirts far removed from the gorgeous emerald green original, have had to warm up to the warbly lament. Talk about pressure.

Smith scored a total of 364 goals for Hibs. Reilly, the last-minute specialist, netted 232 including eighteen hat-tricks. Turnbull hit 199 and many were thundercracks. Ormond, all left foot so they said, bagged 187. And Johnstone hardly stood back at inside-right to admire the finishing of the others – he notched 116.

Today's over-the-top celebrations of over-inked clowns' tap-ins will exist in perpetuity but footage of a goal scored by a member of the quintet is a rare thing. A TV tribute to the Five screened this year unearthed previously unseen film but wasn't able to show even one of those 1,098 goals. This is hugely frustrating if you've been raised on tales of their down-the-slope derring-do, as I was, and longed to see more than just a jittery glimpse of them.

My father, last of the great romantics, went courting with my mother at Easter Road during the Five's pomp. A favourite photograph of my parents comes from a fancy-dress ball. The 'clothes' they're wearing have been cut out of newspaper. Mum is showing a fair bit of leg, being especially proud of pins honed at the Women's League of Health & Beauty, an organisation which I hope wasn't quite as fascistic as it sounds, and Dad is sporting a tie clipped from a back-page headline: 'Tip-top from Smith – Hibs go 1st.'

Dad was Gordon Smith, too, with a facial resemblance and the same black quiff. His favourite tale of the Five, who dovetailed and swapped positions so brilliantly, involved no team-work at all and was the work of just one man: 'the Gay Gordon'. Collecting the ball well inside his own half, Smith embarked on a dream-like sashay, bouncing it off head, knee and foot, then smashing his volley home.

But despite amazing solo goals, stunning team goals, cannonball shots, movie-star looks (Smith), Italian sports cars (and again), friendships with Brigitte Bardot (crikey he gets around), invites to take their sexy football right round the continent and to Brazil as well as a place in the semi-finals of the European Cup, the smashing, absolutely dashing Hibees of the immediate post-Second World War years weren't able to come back from Glasgow with the solid silver trophy 50cm in height and weighing 2.25kg.

In 1947 Hibs were managed by Willie McCartney. 'Frock coat, striped trousers, Homburg hat, carnation – he looked like a circus showman,' recalled Reilly when I met him shortly before he became the last of the Five to pass away in 2013. Hibs' big game of the early rounds was against Rangers: 95,000 shoehorned into Ibrox and victory came in the replay. This would herald the start of a colossal rivalry: the Famous Five versus Rangers' Iron Curtain defence, trading titles before monster crowds.

Though Hibs won three of them in five years Reilly deeply regretted not lifting the cup as it was the great prize of his era, bigger than the league. The old centre-forward seemed to be apologising to the footballers who came after him for cup-shaped expectation which would turn to pressure and eventually become intolerable.

Hibs in '47 were hailed as 'the liveliest and most colourful team of the year' by the *Edinburgh Evening Dispatch* who also declared: 'A final with no west team involved is gay indeed'. The Hibees arrived at Hampden 'singing lustily as though hurling defiance at all-comers,' reported the *Edinburgh Evening News* as chairman Harry Swan told them in 'fatherly tones' that the prestige of the capital was at stake. Rosettes were sold at the rate of 500 per hour.

In front of a crowd of 82,140 Hibs stunned Aberdeen with a goal in just thirty-five seconds, Johnny Cuthbertson the scorer, but the Dons recovered their composure, played a splendid match and deserved a win which 'could have been more emphatic', according to *The Scotsman*. It was a 'real he-man game', said the *Evening News*, with the Hibees gallant but lacking devilment. The afternoon's top performers were Hibs' keeper Jimmy Kerr who produced a 'grand display', according to the paper, and Aberdeen's South African winger Stan Williams. 'His tremendous speed was a heartbreak for the Hibs defenders,' the *Dispatch* admitted.

Kerr saved a penalty but couldn't stop George Hamilton's equaliser from a Williams cross or the latter's winner. The player, who'd guested for Hibs during the war, produced a stunning left-foot finish from a ridiculous angle and Aberdeen for the first time had their hands on the 'coveted piece of silver plate'.

20 April 1958
Clyde 1 Hibernian 0

Just when you think the YouTube trail has gone cold, a clip with the vague title 'Scottish Cup-tie – Rangers vs Hibernian' turns out to be two minutes of the 1951 Ibrox tie watched by a stupendous crowd of 102,342. My father was among them, maybe my mother too, and it's fantastic to finally see Gordon Smith score a goal, the first in the 3-2 victory.

Maybe there are more Smith goals out there, more clips badly captioned and offering no hint of the jewels lying within. Maybe *that* goal is among them – the one-man Edinburgh Tattoo of keepy-uppy magic which has become my votive object, an expression of high football art which may have been embellished by my father (and me), an expression of who I think Hibs are, and a vivid, definite and beautiful link back to Dad even though I have no idea what the goal looked like, how many poor fools Smith bamboozled, how great was the gasp of the crowd when the ball rippled the net.

The goal is my Rosebud. Not Roseburn as in the district of Edinburgh which is rather too close to Tynecastle. Not Roselea as in Smith's junior team when he was a prodigy in Montrose. But Rosebud as in *Citizen Kane*, the great quest and the key to everything. I'd love to find it.

The closest I'd got previously to glimpsing a Smith goal was a Smith sclaff. He even looked majestic when he missed: wonderfully upright with his raven hair flopping in the low winter sun and looking every inch Scotland's first footballing superstar – darting inside from the right wing and bobbling his shot wide. That was against Aberdeen in a 1953 tie, lost 4-3 in another season of high cup promise.

By the final of '58, though, the Five had become Two: Ormond and Turnbull. Johnstone had left for England where he would have more luck in the FA Cup, winning it with Manchester City. Smith, meanwhile, was injured and one knock too many would force Reilly to quit football.

Nevertheless, the ever-loyal *Edinburgh Evening Dispatch* was super-confident. 'Let me state right away that HIBS WILL WIN THE SCOTTISH CUP,' chirruped fan-with-typewriter Jimmy Cowe. A huge Hibee exodus would swell the Hampden crowd to 95,123, even though Paddy Callaghan, a survivor of the victorious 1902 side and nearly eighty, chose to listen to the final at home on his Bakelite. Judging by the Pathe newsreel highlights of the final, an impressive amount of work went into the home-made green-and-white top hats of the young fans down the front of the packed bowl, all of them smiling through the modest dentistry of the time.

That confidence didn't seem to take account of Hibs' injuries, with centre-half Jock Paterson declared unfit in the build-up, and the fact Clyde's entire front five were in the provisional Scotland squad for that summer's World Cup in Sweden. Maybe, after again disposing of Rangers, this time in the semi-final, it was to be Hibs' year after all.

Pre-match entertainment included a cycle pursuit race, an Indian club display sadly not featuring my mother and her Women's League, a schoolgirls' relay and a wrestling bout presumably not involving schoolgirls. A packed programme, and maybe the authorities had anticipated a scrappy wind-battered final, a lucky goal and some dogged defending in protection of it because that was what transpired.

If there was fortune about the winner, though – John Coyle's shot was missing the target before a deflection off John Baxter sent it zinging past goalkeeper Lawrie Leslie – Clyde deserved their victory. The injuries kept on coming for the Hibees, managed by Hugh Shaw, when Ormond and Andy Aitken were hurt. The latter's blazing pace, together with Joe Baker's dead-eye for goals, had encouraged belief among all those apprentice milliners in the Hibs support, but Aitken was crocked early in the game and with no substitutes allowed had to hobble through the rest of it. Even on one leg he managed to cross for Baker whose use of the hand to force the ball over the line – which has the referee point back upfield to signal a goal before doing a double-take and disallowing it – would go down as one of the numerous mini-tragedies of the endless cup melodrama.

'Hard lines Hibernian,' said the *Edinburgh Evening News*, 'and thanks for the fighting effort in the face of misfortune.' *The Scotsman* was equally sympathetic, insisting there was 'much that was admirable in their courageous struggle'. This would be the end of the cup road, as players at least, for Ormond and Turnbull. The paper could not ignore the efforts of the craggy warriors, adding: 'There was something almost moving in their noble failure.'

The *Dispatch*'s verdict? 'Hibs still not interested in the destination of the trophy.'

FOURTEEN

DIMINUTIVE, DARK-HAIRED, DUMPY, THUNDER-THIGHED

6 March 2016
Hibernian 1, Inverness Caley-Thistle 1

WHAT IS IT that Hibs want? Promotion or the Scottish Cup? The question is preoccupying the faithful. Correction: it's driving them absolutely bloody demented.

The prizes are not mutually exclusive. The team could yet achieve both – or end up with neither. So if the fans had to choose one thing, were only allowed one thing, what would it be? It's heart vs head, pragmatism vs romanticism, tomato vs tom-*ay*-to. The grown-up, responsible, five-a-day, drink-in-moderation, pension-plan, relax-o-fit breeks answer would be promotion. But is the right answer not the cup?

It seems reasonable to ask the question. Hibs have lost their last three games in the league, almost certainly ruining their chances of the title. So what if the supporters made a deal with the devil: one more season in the second tier but first they get to be glorious in the cup? Go to Hampden, come back with it. The infernal, infuriating, beautiful cup.

Knowing the fans, who're only too aware that there's many a slip twixt Scottish Cup and lip, they would probably doubt this deal would materialise. Knowing the devil as the supporters think they do, they might suspect he'd renege with a cry of 'Suckers!' before launching into an especially evil rendition of 'Hearts, Hearts, glorious Hearts . . .'

If we're only allowed one thing, Hibbies might say, maybe it should be the League Cup. Hibs just have to win one more game and this trophy will be theirs – the final against Ross County. That would be the easy, safe answer. The Scottish Cup must seem like the difficult, scary, wet-the-bed answer.

Certainly to lift the holey pail Hibs have some way to go. The quarter-final opposition are the other Highland team, Inverness Caley-Thistle, who also happen to be the cup holders, and what a bunch of upstarts they are. ICT's greatest day arrived in what was only the twentieth year of their existence. That hardly seems fair.

ICT and County are a two-pronged teuchter spear, plunged into the heart of the Scottish football establishment. The likes of Hibs, Dunfermline Athletic and St Mirren were part of the natural order who could count on their membership of the top flight being renewed more or less every season. Two of these clubs have fans who can remember Scottish Cup triumphs, a brace of these each, and I think you can guess which two. But the old guard of Fife, Paisley and Leith have had their places taken by sonsy, strapping, wind-burned lads from tenacious, go-ahead outfits located far up the M9. In a reversal of history, ICT and County have enacted football's Lowland Clearances.

This tie is at Easter Road and the visiting manager is well-known around these parts. John Hughes – Yogi to all and sundry – is the Hibs fan who got to live the dream and play for the club. As a growly Desperate Dan-jawed centre-back he was an obvious choice for captain and in 2009 an equally obvious one for boss. But he only lasted a season and a half, his reign typified by a surreal night at Motherwell when Hibs scored six but also conceded six. In his only Scottish Cup campaign, Hibs beat Montrose and also conquered mighty juniors Irvine Meadow, but the big travelling support for a replay at Ross County, not yet a top-flight team, would stagger back to their beds around 2.00 a.m., unable to sleep for another aching disappointment.

*

Inverness are a muscular crew carved in Yogi's image. His Hibs team had more flair although that's probably the Leith perspective you'd expect and of course his ICT have won the cup. For sure his Hibees had Anthony Stokes, a scorer that night in Dingwall, and at Fir Park, but who couldn't quite give his manager the wins he needed. Now Stokes and Hughes, his early mentor, are reacquainted as opponents.

The merest of fan grumblings can now be heard about Stokes. Some supporters instantly bought the idea that he'd have too much class for stout, slow-turning Championship defences and shoot Hibs to the title. This ignored the fact he hadn't played much football and was still striving for sharpness.

He's scored a few times but not the kind of goal he attempts every game: a scuttling run up the inside-left channel, the backing-off defenders bamboozled by what is essentially a flat-footed semi-waddle, then a pass with his right into the far corner of the net.

One thing: he hasn't gelled with Jason Cummings. Both men want to be the main man. Neither wants to defer to, and fluff for, the other. Stokes hasn't stepped down a division to play second fiddle to this cocky toerag with all his own hair. And Cummings is irked that this overgrown bad-boy with a weave has turned up to cramp his style and steal his headlines. They roam the attacking third like hyenas competing to become pack-leader, steering well clear of each other, never passing to each other and being in too much of a hurry to hit their potshots too hard, in the hope this will impress a would-be mate.

At other times watching these two I'm reminded of the Ronald Harwood play *The Dresser* about the camp, bitchy relationship between an actor-manager of mature years who must be addressed as 'Sir' and his long-suffering factotum. But there's no Cummings on this bright, crisp day – he's suspended – so Sir will be partnered by James Keatings.

Whatever the fans' preferences, the club stress their majoring on the league, but the players must be glad whenever cup games against Premiership teams come round. Yes, it's nice to get a breather against the country's better teams, away from the clompy claustrophobia of the Championship's modest middleweights and their do-or-die battle for fifth place.

Three times in six days Hibs have been mugged. Enjoying most of the play has counted for nothing against such committed pests as Morton, Dumbarton and Queen of the South who cram, throttle and deny, then pounce on their rare chances. Top-flight teams don't do two-banks-of-four, at least not against Hibs of the Championship, although maybe they should.

Not that Inverness are the types to stand back and admire Hibs' pleasing passing rhythms and final-third inventiveness. The won't give up their cup without a fight, a bone-juddering challenge from Ross Draper, Caley-Thistle's bow-legged midfield enforcer, being confirmation of this. David Gray is on the receiving end, but the pair shake hands afterwards. Kevin Thomson, though, is angry when Draper then gets down off his exceedingly plump horse and clobbers him. After that Miles Storey and Darren McGregor have a full and frank exchange of views. This tie is a meaty affair and Hughes will be moved to quip that only now and again did some football break out.

Some of the football leaves after just twenty-five minutes when Dylan McGeouch departs injured. This is a common occurrence and an unfortunate one. He's a nice, cool, smooth but determined footballer who strives to strike up the ideal tempo for a game. When he succeeds, and remains on the park long enough, Hibs have their best chance of winning.

The game is exciting, though, and Gray and Liam Fontaine force desperate saves from ICT goalkeeper Owain Fon Williams. Meanwhile Mark Oxley is spreading anxiety through the Famous Five Stand behind his goal with his Dracula-like aversion to the cross. The fans have always known this about him, but don't like to be reminded too often. Unfortunately three Inverness corners do just that. Oxley is a strapping fellow with a pleasingly thick Yorkshire accent and maybe the latter is utilised in his shot-stopping which is a strong aspect of his game – but is he too well-groomed? That hair and beard look like they require a fair bit of attention in the morning. If you've known scruffy, half-shut-knife goalies like Alan Rough, bandy and toothless ones like Jim Leighton and tracky-bummed ones such as Hamish McAlpine, you're probably unnerved by The Ox and his best-a-man-can-get appearance – although no one's suggesting he keeps a ladies' vanity mirror in the back of the net.

It's a ding-dong first half. Hibs are keen to win the tie today because a replay would have to come right after the League Cup final. Their urgency leaves plenty of opportunity for Inverness to roar upfield on the counter-attack. But there's more than a hint that Stokes and Keatings – aware of each other's movements, interested in them – could develop a simpatico relationship.

Where have all the striker double-acts gone? Like comedy double-acts they're no longer commonplace. It used to be that all clubs played a pair of forwards, now most go with just the one, while in comedy it's a solitary stand-up yakking about himself all night, earning a small fortune, blowing it up his egomaniacal nose. The best up-front love-in I ever witnessed on the old Easter Road slope was between the tall, slim, blond, debonair Alan Gordon and the diminutive, dark-haired, dumpy, thunder-thighed Jimmy O'Rourke – the go-to guys for goals in Turnbull's Tornadoes.

Their success wasn't really down to uncanny telepathy, though the mutual respect and appreciation was obvious. They were simply very good players surrounded by lots of other very good players, the latter providing the duo with bountiful scoring opportunities of great variety. There were more than enough goals to go round in that side, and these two didn't grab more than their fair share, though it's definitely true that O'Rourke slid his short, fat, hairy legs across the turf to rob his captain Pat Stanton of the sixth of the seven Hibs scored against Hearts on New Year's Day, 1973.

If this was a comedy double-act and not a football one then you'd have thought Gordon came from the Cambridge Footlights and O'Rourke the world of custard-pie slapstick. One liked to sculpt and finesse his goals while the other cheerfully bundled his into the net. O'Rourke was a Hibee fanatic who if he hadn't played for the club would have been a terrace bauchle, revelling in seven-nil for the rest of his life, pausing only occasionally to wonder if the club would ever achieve anything to top it. Gordon, who'd played for Hearts previously, was that rare thing: a footballer with a university degree. 'The trouble with you, Gordon,' growled Eddie Turnbull, possibly after an intellectual challenge to the disciplinarian manager's demands, 'is that all your brains are in your heid!' But the fans loved the aesthete and the artisan equally, and really hoped they could have fired Hibs to glory.

The first tie I saw absolutely convinced me Hibs were going to win the cup. That was 1971's 8-1 thumping of Forfar Athletic where O'Rourke, who'd previously operated in the shadows of ruthless men, serious goal-grabbers like Colin Stein and Joe McBride, bagged a hat-trick. First tie, and also my first hat-trick. I brought all of my thirteen-year-old insight and perception to bear on the matter: this was going to be the year. In the two previous seasons Hibs had drawn Rangers away in the first round, losing both times. This time they would progress in the competition, meeting Rangers in the semis. Same outcome.

In 1972 Gordon arrived, just in time for another cup adventure, scoring his first goal for his new club in the third round at Partick Thistle, a game really remembered for the other strike by Erich Schaedler, son of a German prisoner-of-war. This was a shot from way out left after a throw-in came back to him that was positively Argentinian in its audaciousness.

Maybe Gordon was the man to enable O'Rourke to properly flourish. In the following rounds, the new partnership took it in turns to find the net, a gentlemanly arrangement which propelled Hibs all the way to the final. Gordon scored at Hampden, Celtic briefly quivered and then romped to a 6-1 victory.

The following season at the quarter-final stage, my father and I got into Ibrox just in time to see Gordon soar above the Rangers defence, above even Peter McCloy, the unfeasibly lofty goalkeeper nicknamed the Girvan Lighthouse, to bullet a header into the net. This was well into the second half, our lateness the result of Dad locking the car with the keys still in the ignition. He would hammer the window with a rock for many minutes, perturbing no one on the mean streets of the stadium environs. Two cup optimists reckoned being present for the goal was a good omen for the replay. That game attracted the second-biggest Easter Road throng for which I'd had the scary pleasure of being semi-asphyxiated on the Bothwell Street footbridge – 49,007. The combined gate for both matches was 102,994, a lot of people to see Hibs ultimately fail again.

O'Rourke and Gordon, funnier than Little and Large, Cannon and Ball and Mike and Bernie Winters put together without cracking a single gag, would get back in the old routine for one last cup campaign. In 1974 Jimmy bumped and barged his way to a hat-trick against Kilmarnock and Alan matched the feat in painterly fashion in the next round with Dundee the opposition. Could *this* be the year? Alas no. Our duo had seemed improbable on paper. Ah but football wasn't played on paper in the early 1970s; it was enacted on mudheaps strewn with toilet-roll or on ice-rinks with an orange ball. Gordon and O'Rourke were a dream double-act but still it wasn't enough.

Meanwhile, Stokes and Keatings are getting along rather well, waving and blowing kisses when one of them is forced wide by Hibs' efforts to win the tie – then reuniting in the middle with manly grapples which threaten to turn into an Olly Reed-Alan Bates wrestling match. It's a bromance, it's a strike partnership, or it seems that way compared with Stokes' efforts to get along with Cummings, who's sat in the West Stand in impossibly tight jeans playing with his hair and his smartphone but must be impressed.

Keatings stays close to Stokes, studying his movement, loving his work, but in the first half he's too keen to finish off a dynamic piece of play by Stokes who bursts into the box to shoot across Fon Williams, the keeper fingertipping the effort onto a post where his sidekick is lurking, only to be flagged for offside.

But in the second half the intimacy pays off when Stokes, who's been trying to cause small, controlled explosions around the ICT box, sparks the move of the match. An excitable Hibby would call it tiki-taki: Stokes, twenty yards out, demands Keatings' involvement in a one-two despite heavy congestion. When he gets the ball back he nonchalantly pops it to Gray hurtling down the right. The wing-back's hard, low cross is banged home by Keatings whose gleeful expression while seeking out the chief architect can be interpreted thus: 'Hey, how did I do?'

Until that moment some fans were maybe about to give up on the cup for another season. I know I was. Hibs had too much else going on and the league, promotion, had to be their heart's desire. Let's be grown up about this. But, hang on, who want to be sensible? If the team can just get through today, then just get through the semi-final, then just get through the final . . .

Supporters are so persuadable. One goal, admittedly a very good one, and reason and logic are ejected from the ground, slapped with lifetime bans. It's back on. The dream lives. Why did we ever doubt this team? Whoever's turn it is to fetch the pies I'll have two. Happy Hibby days.

Hibs could do with a second goal but when it doesn't come they consolidate. There's no shame in this – even the great Barcelona will throw down a few sandbags towards the end of a game – but the team are looking a bit wabbit. They put a lot into overcoming Hearts. Then came those stumbles in the league. Inverness have been urgent, clanking opponents and Hibs have stood up to the challenge, playing some clever football when the breathless action allowed, but now they seem to have nothing left. Caley-Thistle flex their muscles for a final assault and there's a creeping inevitability about the equaliser twelve minutes from the end.

John Hughes throws on his substitutes, handing lanky Congolese striker Andrea Mbuyi-Mutombo a note. Yogi will joke afterwards that this was simply a shopping list – 'My messages for tonight: two bags of potatoes and a half-loaf' – but the changes do the trick with Mbuyi-Mutombo shooting high into the net after fellow sub Lewis Horner was able to surge through a puggled Hibs defence and cross from the byline. Inverness have grabbed a replay, they're still in the cup, and in their relief Yogi yanks down his goalscorer's shorts.

It's a wacky end to hectic tie but for Hibs a crazy season has just got crazier. Three days after the League Cup final they must reconvene against Inverness in the Highlands. Get through that one – and how difficult will it be to raise themselves if they lose at Hampden? – then they will in all likelihood have to play two games a week until the end of the season. There will be a league backlog. Then, almost certainly, the playoffs for promotion. And then there will be the Scottish Cup final, should they make it, although this seems quite far away now.

One more thing about Alan Gordon: when he started at Hearts he was still at school, George Heriot's, one of Edinburgh's best. He was selected to travel to Milan for an Inter-Cities Fairs Cup-tie against the mighty Inter and although not expected to play, it was going to be great experience and, he thought, something the school might view as an honour. But Heriot's was a rugby establishment and the masters disapproved of football, an oikish sport which had enabled the teenager to buy a car every bit as good as theirs. When the young prospect asked the head if he could be excused lessons for a couple of days he was told: 'Snap out of it, Gordon, this just won't do. I don't want the whole of the fifth form trooping along here claiming they've got pressing business in Italy simply because they fancy a skive.'

It was almost as if the school dismissed him as a fantasist whose ambition in life would never be fulfilled. After this tie, with Hibs' best chance seeming to have gone, some fans are probably ready to accept this as a description of themselves.

FIFTEEN

'STOKESY RECKONED THE CHAMPIONSHIP WAS THE HARDEST LEAGUE. DEFENDERS WANTED TO KICK HIM . . . BECAUSE HE WAS ANTHONY STOKES'

ALAN STUBBS PONDERS the issue which at one point Hibs fans worried might stymie the season: the problematic relationship between Jason Cummings and Anthony Stokes. 'On the training pitch there honestly wasn't a problem; they got on really well together,' he says. 'Maybe the chemistry for a strike partnership wasn't quite there. Perhaps Stokesy coming in took a bit of the limelight away from Jason.'

Stubbs thought long and hard before taking Stokes on loan. 'We had a good group. Was I worried about the harmony being disrupted? Of course. I had to be concerned about Anthony off the pitch and we did need to have one or two conversations to make sure his lifestyle was right. Nothing bad, just in terms of relationships. His marriage was breaking up and there were children involved. He was having to deal with that, rush back to Ireland a few times, and I told him he shouldn't suffer in silence and that the club would try to help. There was a lot more to Anthony's time at Hibs than met the eye. I always think he's one of these guys continually having to answer questions, sometimes unjustifiably so.

'One thing which wasn't in question was Anthony's ability and from day one back at Hibs he knew what he had to do. His time at Celtic was coming to an end and he needed to earn a new contract somewhere else. He came to us, trained really well and his willingness to do the best he could for Hibs was always there. He did say to me a few times how much tougher the Championship was compared with the Premiership. He had less time on the ball and defenders wanted to kick him more. Because he was Anthony Stokes, basically.'

Against Inverness-Caley Thistle, Stubbs agrees that Stokes and James Keatings chimed. 'Keats looks to play as a partner whereas Jason is an individual. It's his ball, basically. I don't think Jason will mind me saying this but Keats is more experienced and therefore more intelligent about the striker's job in totality. It isn't just about scoring goals, although that is the most important aspect.'

Stubbs knew Hibs were in for a testing afternoon. 'They were the type of team we hadn't faced an awful lot – really big. We knew they'd be physical and try and dominate with set-pieces and by firing the ball into our box. But we scored a good goal and probably should have got a second. Chance gone? No, I just thought it was an opportunity missed.'

Okay, so how soon after leaving Hibs did Stubbs miss Cummings? 'Personality-wise? Right away. He's an infectious character. He wasn't a handful. Daft, for sure, but in a nice way.'

SIXTEEN

'THE REFEREE, BRIAN MCGINLEY, WASN'T GOING TO GIVE UP THE BEACH FOR ANY MORE OF THIS ESCHER-LIKE EXPLORATION OF INFINITY . . .'

SO THERE WE were at Nutbush City Limits. Or, more accurately and less romantically, the western outskirts of Edinburgh, the prim suburb of Corstorphine, and the Securex building with the clock on the wall. 'Durex HQ,' my father would say every time we set off, his eldest son still too young to get the joke. This was where the classic route to Hampden began.

We didn't live close to Rubberjohnny House but it was here that we left Edinburgh behind. We didn't support a team qualifying for enough Scottish Cup finals which would have qualified the route as classic, but no matter: in 1972 Hibs had a fine side and the best, my father assured me, since the days of the Famous Five. One of them, Eddie Turnbull, was now the manager, intent on making the Hibees a force in the land, worrying the Old Firm, intent on seizing their entitlement silverware.

I did not dress like fans get kitted out for finals now, with every item of clothing the colour of their team, topped off with facepainted flags and a fire-hazard wig. My Hibs scarf was too long to tie round a wrist, bovver boy-style, and anyhow I didn't have the balls for that. To be honest the scarf – knitted by my mother and better suited to a university campus ladykiller although I didn't have the balls for that either – had been ditched completely since some Rangers fans tried to garotte me with it on my first visit to Ibrox the previous year. My father looked as he always looked: long silver hair under a John Lennon cap, dark blue leather jacket tied with a belt. This was his garb for interviewing great Scots of the cultural panoply such as macho moviemaker Alan Sharp and lady of letters Muriel Spark and it was his garb for the football.

My hair was long, too, modelled on the bangs of Alex Cropley, the grooviest player in the Hibs team and maybe all Scotland at that time. There was a tremendous day at the Edinburgh boutique Jean Machine when, as Cropley was exiting – possibly with a scoop-necked, bell-sleeved, tie-dye T-shirt and, no, I wouldn't have been able to carry that off either – he held open the Wild West saloon-style swing-doors for me. Tragically Cropley wasn't playing at Hampden, having been crocked by Alex Ferguson at his late-career grumpiest playing for Falkirk a few weeks before. The big showdown with Celtic wasn't a tremendous day, Hibs losing by the joint biggest margin in the history of the competition.

How did it get to 6-1? Billy McNeill scored right away, as the Hibees were still settling into their first final for fourteen years, but Alan Gordon equalised ten minutes later. Celtic regained the lead before half-time although Hibs were still very much in the game. The second half featured some outstanding attacking play from both sides but only Celtic's finishing was devastating, Lou Macari adding a double to Dixie Deans' hat-trick.

It seems like a typically Hibee response to suggest my team were unlucky. Slumped on the red blaes slopes of Hampden at the end, I was probably wondering how you went about requesting a re-match. I was devastated. This was as good a side as Hibs could muster and I'd just watched them being thrashed.

But I didn't think then that I'd still be waiting for the cup by the

Follow that. The 1902 cup winning team relax into the task of haunting their successors. *Scran*

The 1924 final was a diamond day for the greatest-ever Airdrie team who vanquished Hibs 2-0. *Old Scottish Football*

Hibs didn't concede a goal all the way to the 1923 final but long-trousered officialdom would record a 1-0 triumph for Celtic.

The Second World War meant it would be eight years before the final was contested again and in 1947 Hibs needed just 35 seconds to race into the lead – but Aberdeen won the cup with an outrageous shot from South African winger Stan Williams.

Eddie Turnbull captained Hibs to the 1958 final on a wave of great expectancy but Clyde, led by Harry Haddock, were to kipper them. *The Scotsman Archives*

Hibs in 1958 on the way to more Hampden heartache. All but one of the ten final defeats would come in the great bowl. *The Scotsman Archives*

Bearing flags and favours, fathers and sons smile hopefully before the 1972 final. Hibs would crash to a record-equalling defeat for the cup showpiece. *The Scotsman Archives*

Dixie Deans completes his famous hat-trick in Celtic's 1972 thrashing of Hibs and is about to embark on his notorious somersault celebration. *Scottish News and Sport*

The interminable 1979 final exhausted some, including the referee who left for his summer holidays before the third instalment, witnessed by just 30,602. *The Scotsman Archives*

'I know this has already gone on for ever, lads, but just half an hour more and we could be holding more than teacups.' Eddie Turnbull's extra-time urgings in the *War and Peace* Final. *The Scotsman Archives*

It's a majestic diving header fit to win the cup . . . but unfortunately Arthur Duncan scored at the wrong end in 1979 to hand the trophy to Rangers. *The Scotsman Archives*

Celtic shattered Hibs' cup dreams in five finals and in 2001 Henrik Larsson was the arch-tormentor, scoring two goals. *Getty Images*

Many Hibs fans had exited Hampden – some to avoid answering the phone or the front door all summer, others to join the Foreign Legion – after Rudi Skacel scored the fifth and last Hearts goal in 2012's Auld Reekie Deathmatch. *Getty Images*

The background of big metal boxes and bored polis may be an unpromising one but all successful cup quests have to start somewhere and it was a fan-turned-player, Darren McGregor, who set Hibs on the road to glory with this sizzling strike at Raith Rovers. *SNS*

Paul Hanlon, Hibby through and through, shows his delight at scoring the stoppage-time equaliser against Hearts. He thought this feeling couldn't be topped. It could. *Evening Times*

Touch of an angel, though occasionally an angel riding a donkey, Hearts reject Jason Cummings boots his old club out of the cup. *SNS Group*

James Keatings, who had to bide his time during the cup run, grabbed his chance against Inverness Caley-Thistle to finish off a fine team goal and is congratulated by Liam Henderson. *Getty Images*

The unlikeliest of cup triumphs produced the most improbable of heroes when emergency goalkeeper Conrad Logan – the Polar Bear – played his first game for 16 months and saved the penalties which sent Hibs to the final. *Getty Images*

A team which would play with flair, a side to make the fans proud again – these were Alan Stubbs' stated aims when he arrived at Hibs. He had something else in mind as well . . . *Getty Images*

Captain David Gray celebrates his hoodoo-busting, curse-smashing, jinx-trumping winner.
Getty Images

A sight Hibs fans thought they'd never see and which many weren't able to stay alive for – the hoisting of the cup. *Getty Images*

There's sunshine on Leith Street as the victory parade, witnessed by 150,000, leaves uptown behind and heads into the port where they swear by the motto 'Persevered'. *Getty Images*

time I'd reached my mother's age when she died. I was young and not yet entrammelled into work, responsibilities and the sensible, practical thinking required of adulthood. I was still able to dream. Plus I had my father telling me not to worry, it was going to be alright. In a card on my next birthday he put a sub-editor's pencil through the Hallmark slush so it read: ' . . . And they will win it.'

I still have the card, with the d of the 'And' curvy-backed like it's suffering from lumbago. The sequence of cartoon images on it are of father-son bonding untypical of the time and certainly of our household, but I wouldn't have wanted Dad to be all sweatshirty-matey with me like fathers are supposed to behave now. It was enough that he took me to the football and on all those Scottish Cup misadventures.

Maybe the M8 motorway was quite gloomy in 1972 but who needed roadside art and the Harthill pie-stop renamed Heart of Scotland when you had the Texaco Scottish Football Routemaster on your lap, the Beatles on the eight-track cartridge, hope in your heart and the wisdom of my designated driver speculating that Alex Edwards, our playmaker before the title existed, could probably chip a ball and make it land on a newly-redundant threepenny bit? My only regret about these trips is that they weren't in the Lotus F2 racing-car or the Riley with the runner-boards or any of the other hopelessly and wonderfully unsuitable motors Dad used to own.

Edwards wasn't quite as brilliant as Jimmy Johnstone in that final. Bobby Murdoch was better than Pat Stanton and George Connelly was better than John Blackley who threw his runners-up medal across the Hampden car park just after Turnbull had told his shell-shocked men to allow the defeat to linger and hurt and then learn from it.

'We'll be back,' Turnbull growled and Hibs returned to Hampden seven months later to beat Celtic to win the League Cup, Edwards chipping the ball over the defensive wall and making it land on Stanton's toe for the opening goal.

Just as the Scottish Cup final of 1947 possibly came too early for the Hibs team in which Turnbull played – the Famous Five were not quite fully formed – so 1972 may have been premature for the side he was building as manager. But when you're Hibs in the cup you have to grab your chances; they don't come round too often. As Easter Road boss Turnbull would get one more chance – the *War and Peace* Final of 1979.

Three times Hibs and Rangers squared up to each other. The first game was a typical sunshiney Saturday in May with the customary Hampden showpiece frills led by massed pipe bands although the SFA did acknowledge the existence of other forms of music that year and allowed Scotland's Middle of the Road to be birled round the pitch on the back of a coal lorry. The combo, led by the hot-panted Sally Carr, may have performed their prog-rock classic 'Chirpy Chirpy Cheep Cheep' more than once.

By the third game, though, the scene had changed markedly. It was a dank Monday night, rain hammering down on a much smaller crowd heading for the stadium, everyone with their coat collars turned up and looking furtive and mildly desperate. As part of the build-up to the first match we were also treated to polis manoeuvres with King the Alsatian jumping through flaming hoops and nabbing pretend baddies. The third attempt at settling the competition was more suggestive of a dog-fighting contest, a sinister event with no fanfare, no lingering outside to savour the atmosphere, possibly no advertising that it was even taking place.

Look on YouTube where all the filmed finals are stored and you won't find any footage of this one: not the first game (0-0), nor the second (same scoreline, after extra-time) nor the third. This is the closest Hibs have come to winning the cup and yet it's like their efforts were all in vain.

Arthur Duncan, the hurtling winger who seemed like he could run for ever, had retreated to left-back and was the only survivor from the

'72 team. In the intervening years Turnbull had tried to harden Hibs so they'd be less likely to be bullied by the Old Firm but in '79 he still found room for Ally MacLeod and Ralph Callachan, two languorous midfielders who played in smoking jackets, and a university lad, Colin Campbell, who almost won the Hibees the dour first game, but Rangers' keeper Peter McCloy Kung Fu-ed him and amazingly no penalty was given. Then in the dying minutes the totem-pole goalie used his ridiculously unfair height advantage to keep out a Campbell drive.

Hibs could have won the second game, too. Rangers no longer made the earth shake. Towards the end of the Willie Waddell era, they were losing some of their awesome power and Hibs would occasionally win. Jock Wallace's side, it's true, were tremor-causing, Treble-devourers, but in '79 John Greig's team featured Gordon Smith with a *Summertime Special* backing dancer's blow-dry. Somewhat less intimidating, then.

Could Hibs do it at the third time of asking? Because of the interminable length of the final they'd shed any lingering nervousness. On and on it went, without goals and seemingly without end. As Dad and I travelled back and forth along the classic route, the experience of watching our team try to win the cup became like work, duty, a penance.

And then suddenly someone scored. It was Hibs' Tony Higgins, a lumbering giant who stomped between midfield and attack, between effectiveness and comedy. His delicate work on the ball would often astonish; it was like you were watching a Tyrannosaurus Rex knit. When T.Hig found the net the Hibs fans, who'd forgotten what a goal looked like, were silent for a few seconds and then they roared. The Rangers fans were possibly roaring inside because suddenly this final mattered again. TV had given up on it, likewise the impartial fan. It had been ghettoised, banished and forgotten about by everyone except 30,602 nutters. The third game was delayed until after the Home Internationals, the traditional season finale, when football usually went on holiday. Brian McGinley, who refereed the first two games, wasn't going to give up the beach for any more of this Escher-like exploration of infinity and so handed the job to Ian Foote.

That wasn't a classic Ibrox team by any means but they did have Derek Johnstone, a bubble-permed brute whose bulleted headers were harder than most players' shots. He got Rangers level then he put them ahead.

Then MacLeod, who was one of my father's favourite players by dint of his debonair volleys and funny, short-paced scuttle, equalised and almost restored Hibs' advantage. The endless final was providing different possible outcomes every few minutes. And then came the brilliant winner, as thrilling a diving header as you could ever wish to see, but unfortunately Arthur Duncan put the ball through his own net.

What a way to lose. If one of the two sides which Turnbull steered to Hampden could have won the cup then I would rather it had been the '72 version. But the '79 side would have been worthy winners as characters abounded in MacLeod, Callachan, snarling captain George Stewart, that fine sweeper Jackie McNamara, Duracell-powered Des Bremner in the midfield and 'Benny' Brazil who was never very Brazilian but tried hard. Brazil seemed to sum up Hibs' Hampden ill-fortune when, as a bus driver after quitting playing, he volunteered to pilot the open-top coach for the winners of the 2003 League Cup final because he couldn't see Livingston beating the Hibees – but they did.

The cruellest blow, though, befell Duncan. He probably wanted the gates to be opened after his soaring own goal so he could sprint right out of the stadium. Last anyone knew, Arthur was somewhere in the antipodes.

Some of the quests organised by my father had a successful outcome. The earliest one I can remember was a search for the source of the buzzing sound which had intrigued this five-year-old country boy.

'Come on, we'll find it,' he said, leading me across a couple of fields which to me seemed like several counties, ending up at the scene of mass tree-felling. He said these words with the calm, wise certainty with which he'd later write: '. . . And they will win it.' But how was that ever going to happen? A great Hibs side couldn't win the cup and a good one had been desperately unlucky.

Desperately sad in '79, as well as desperately drookit, I thought about reminding him of his birthday-card message and how it didn't seem so reassuring anymore. But as we said our farewells to Mount Florida, shot of it at last, we made a concerted effort to move the conversation away from football, Hibs and the cup and into less traumatic and tragic areas and more trivial ones, like what I was going to do with the rest of my life.

Though we'd return to Hampden for other occasions, my father and I never got to travel the classic route in the Scottish Cup again before he died. The three-in-one final, forgotten by many, hasn't been easy to shake for those who witnessed it. I can't shake it yet, for when I search eBay for old match programmes the one from '79 pops up every time. There's Derek Johnstone on the front cover, leering at me. He seems to be saying: 'Is that final over yet? What was the score?'

SEVENTEEN

YE OLDE FIERY SPHERES

16 March 2016
Inverness Caley-Thistle 1, Hibernian 2

JASON CUMMINGS WANTED to chuck himself off a bridge. For Darren McGregor it was the worst moment of his life. So what must Liam Fontaine have felt when, in the ninetieth minute, he mis-kicked horribly to hand the League Cup to Ross County?

This was a first-ever trophy for a team from a town with a population of 5,491, making them the most modestly-appointed winners of one of the top prizes. There's losing big matches and there's doing it the Hibs way. The campaign for 'Hibsing it' to be formally admitted into the language just received another huge spike.

Fontaine took to Twitter to apologise to the fans for his error: 'I made a mistake and killed my dream of lifting this cup for a club I love.' He spoke of dealing with the disappointment, moving on quickly. But surely the replay in the other cup has come around too soon for the team. And maybe on the journey to Inverness it will be wise to seat Cummings furthest from the coach door, just in case he spots the Kessock Bridge and is still in flyin'-heidy mode.

It wouldn't be hard for Hibs' record in the League Cup to be better than their achievements in the Scottish Cup, and the improvement is only marginal. The score for the number of times silverware has been hoisted stands at League Cup 3, Scottish Cup 2. The League Cup has only been in existence for sixty-nine years, less than half the longevity of the Scottish Cup, which might make three wins sound slightly more impressive. Maybe in your Wee Red Book, pal; not in mine.

Nevertheless I was fortunate to bear witness to the trio of triumphs in the lesser competition, the 'diddy cup' as Hearts fans would have it. These Hampden days are what Kenneth Clark on *Civilisation* – or maybe it was Davina McCall on *Big Brother* – would have called my 'best bits'. They would fit easily on a football version of a donor card tucked in a leatherette wallet in the event of a fatal accident. Instead of vital organs the card would list vital memories: these were mine but they're no use to me now, please look after them.

The first League Cup, in 1972, was 2-1 against Jock Stein's Celtic, the apogee of Turnbull's Tornadoes. The Pat Stanton final. The blackest December day lit up by a man with a brilliantly solid knitting-pattern model haircut and a brilliantly upright brigadier's disposition, save for his habit of prodding the ball forward with hen's toes, like every cocky, keelie product of Edinburgh's hard-knocks Niddrie estate. And the brilliant pop tune from that winter which always reminds me of the Tornadoes is Python Lee Jackson's 'In a Broken Dream'. Winning the Scottish Cup, too, seemed within this flair-filled side's grasp but it didn't happen.

The second League Cup, in 1991, was the regeneration of a broken team. The then Hearts chairman, rotund Thatcherite bon viveur Wallace Mercer, tried to merge the two Edinburgh clubs. Correction: Wallet Merger tried to put Hibs out of business. Some spiv wine-bar tycoons in charge at Easter Road at the time almost achieved that through their own incompetence. Resistance was mobilised and Mercer had to admit defeat, being stunned by the sheer scale and passion of the Leith revolt. The side assembled by

Alex Miller – less swashbuckling than the Tornadoes but then most were – beat Dunfermline Athletic 2-0 thanks mainly to the deedle-dawdle of the pocket-sized playmaker Mickey Weir.

The third League Cup – I know, I know, it's not quite the climax of Philip Roth's *American Trilogy* or the third series of *The Wire* – was won in 2007 with a team of bright young things which John Collins inherited from Tony Mowbray. After Turnbull's Tornadoes, they're probably Easter Road's favourite team of the past fifty years. Some fans would have liked the Hibs fans in the side – Derek Riordan, Garry O'Connor and Kevin Thomson – to have stayed long enough for that triumph, their exotic-bird haircuts being emblematic of the era, but no one could deny that the chromedome centre-back Rob Jones and Moroccan striker Abdessalam 'Benji' Benjelloun didn't bring character and vim. Kilmarnock were hammered 5-1 and the French playmaker Guillaume Beuzelin, a beautifully unhurried footballer, ran the show all in his own sweet time.

Of course the League Cup has brought woe. It's been a different kind of woe to that of the Scottish Cup because the League Cup is a trophy we occasionally wake in sunshine and think we could win, as opposed to torture ourselves nightly, get all twisted up in the bedcovers, over the ongoing failure. League Cup disappointment includes five defeats in the final. Twice Hibs were hit by Celtic for six and on another occasion took 30,000 expectant fans to Hampden only to lose witlessly to Livingston. There was a dismal semi-final capitulation against Ayr United which helped bring about the end of Franck Sauzee's *bon vacances* in Leith as well as that time in Montrose when a biblical storm blew these scaly, gnarly, hard-tackling beasties right out of the North Sea and onto a tiny park. The Gable Endies – the best nickname in football – removed another much-fancied green-and-white XI from the competition.

Just the latest to let down the tyres on Hibs' open-top bus, Ross County didn't murder Alan Stubbs' side in the final, nothing like.

They were well-organised and gutsy and not shy about hitting the stands and content to wait for their moment, but Hibs played most of the football. This is how Stubbs' team tend to lose in big games. They don't decline to show up or play like wimps. They can be unlucky. But all of this is irrelevant to the Hearts fans lobbying the *OED*. You blow a game, you've Hibsed it.

Now everyone is using the term and no one seems to care about subtle distinctions. Newspapers slow to pick up on the Jambo campaign rush to use the phrase as often as possible. Every defeat and there's been a few recently has been a case of the team Hibsing it, even when they hadn't actually held an advantage. This would drive you insane if you weren't already a lunatic follower of Hibernian FC, being carefully tracked by a yellow van.

Ross County scored first in the final but the hapless Fontaine equalised and while Hibs dominated possession they were impatient and, after the grind of games recently, somewhat frazzled. There was still a disconnect between Stokes and Cummings, the latter being restored to the side after his suspension but continuing to appear half-irritated by Stokes' presence and half-intimidated. He shot when he should have passed and passed when he should have belted it. His goals have dried up since Stokes' arrival and the latter isn't scoring either.

So the 20,000 Hibs fans at Hampden for this latest let-down – the eleventh defeat in fifteen visits since 2000 – packed up and headed for home. Through the Gorbals, the former world heritage slum, and past the oldest house in Glasgow and the various pubs competing for being the oldest boozer. Onto the M8 and past the Lanarkshire church beckoning bleakly from a blasted hilltop where, who knows, they might have the answer to an urgent, 114-year-old sporting conundrum. Then past the carriageway culture: the Teletubbies tower, the grass pyramids and the purple sheep, and on into 'mine own romantic town', Sir Walter Scott's description of Edinburgh, glancing only fleetingly at the Maybury roundabout where the roofless charabanc parks up for a victorious team that rarely keeps its appointment.

The theme of the radio babble on the journey is that Hibs' big season – the biggest for years – is far from done. 'Still loads to play for,' the pundits insist. There's the promotion bid, now requiring the playoffs, and there's the Scottish Cup. But more than a few fans are starting to fear, as their song says, that hearts will be broken (again). They can see, and appreciate, that Hibs put on a good show in key games now, that the faffing fecklessness of the past has gone. 'Still loads to play for,' repeat the blether-merchants. But it's difficult to share this optimism.

*

Inverness isn't one of Hibs' favourite places. So the air is clean, the accents melodious and you can spot dolphins in the Moray Firth beyond the ground – so bloody what? Hibs can't win there, or they couldn't, not for a long time.

Both Highland teams, ICT and Ross County, enjoy the fact that the rest of Scottish football views them as a northerly irritation much like the midge. They know that clubs from the Central Belt hate the three-to-four-hour slog and so they maximise their remoteness. And for long enough it was reckoned that Hibs, more than most, started to feel queasy at the first sight of the snow-gates as their coach rumbled towards Drumochter Pass.

Terry Butcher, before his ill-starred spell at Easter Road, was one of the Highland bosses who regularly performed rain dances for Hibee visits. 'When Hibs came up to Inverness I always hoped it would be windy, wet, cold and horrible,' he once told me. 'We were used to the bad weather – they never fancied it. They seemed to have a block about coming to the Highlands and we always just got stuck into them.' Although Hibs did eventually break their far-north hoodoo they've continued to tread warily through the heather, lest they be tripped up by a grouchy stag, a flying haggis with lousy radar, the Loch Ness Monster or something equally long and curvy and dreadful like one of Ross Draper's legs.

The Tulloch Caledonian Stadium is modern so inevitably it requires fans to leave the town behind for a trek to the outskirts. The road from the throbbing pulsebeat of Inversnecky winds unpromisingly past goods yards. Most newish grounds would be perfectly at home in such a setting and viewed from the outside this one is no different from others on the Scottish fitbascape, either resembling a light industrial warehouse or a retail pile-'em-high. But in one aspect it effortlessly outstrips the rest – the windchill. This strips out your cheeks, removing whole layers of skin.

This must be the coldest ground in Britain although I wouldn't go as far as to call the city of Inverness godforsaken. The first time I visited, with a girlfriend in the 1980s, we were turned away by five bed-and-breakfast landladies in a row because the good Lord would have been 'awfa vexed' at the idea of us slipping between their best and most electrically-charged Terylene as an unmarried couple. For this game on a Wednesday night the welcome mat is a swampy covering of thick haar and, really and truly, this looks for all the world like a place where cup dreams come to die.

Caley-Thistle manager and ex-Hibee John Hughes offers sympathy to his old team for their Hampden disappointment. He's one of many one-time Easter Road bosses to win the cup, just not when he was at Hibs. Others include Eddie Turnbull, Alex McLeish, Bobby Williamson and Jock Stein, who achieved eight triumphs at Celtic. Yogi the Leither would love to see Hibs win the trophy eventually, but not this year, and he has a fiendish plan. ICT weren't exactly diminutive first time round, but Hughes has mustered his biggest men for the rematch. There are no less than eight Gullivers on the pitch, all well over 6ft, and an entirely predictable aerial bombardment begins immediately. High looping crosses are catapulted towards Mark Oxley who was jittery at Easter Road and presumably isn't too enamoured by the deliveries now dropping onto him from the cold sea mist.

But he's got help. Fontaine and Darren McGregor are trying to neutralise these missiles before they reach their goalkeeper. McGregor has been on consistently combative and committed form for a while now; Fontaine is being true to his tweet and trying to make up for that fatal fluff three days before. Together they climb and stretch and clear.

'Brilliant, Margo!' is the shout when it's Fontaine doing the clearing. 'And again, Margo!' Like McGregor and Marvin Bartley, Fontaine is thirtysomething or thereabouts, been around a bit, performed in some apologetic arenas, developed the sound attitude of a late-career pro who knows he won't get too many more opportunities and is viewed by Stubbs as important ballast for a side which looks for flair from its young players who can of course be inconsistent. He may not quite have Dame Margo's prima-ballerina poise but his goal against Ross County was still a nimble turn and volley and he almost equalised in the last minute with that rare thing, a centre-back's overhead kick.

This is the kind of night, and ICT the kind of opposition, which would have done for Hibs in previous cup campaigns. Inverness are so northerly and dastardly that they bring to mind the sieges which that kids' TV genius Oliver Postgate's character Noggin the Nog used to have to endure from a high turret occupied by his sworn enemy Nogbad the Bad. Noggin was shy and borderline timid, which is widely regarded as Hibs' natural disposition, but the men in green-and-white are facing down the challenge and David Gray is playing a captain's part in helping repel the steepling dangers posed by ICT. Like Dylan McGeouch, who's missing after breaking down in the first game, Gray is fragile. The sight of the wing-back lying crumpled in a heap, failing to respond to the tender mercies of physiotherapist Kitty Forrest, has become all too familiar. The Hibs fans who've filled the South Stand in good numbers don't want a repeat tonight because his muscular drive is important to the team and they wouldn't mind seeing a goal from the skipper.

Gray doesn't score often but strikes usually come against Rangers, are often crackers and invariably vital. The supporters are probably thinking, with Stokes sizzling a shot into the side-netting, a familiar outcome at the moment, that they'll have to look elsewhere for a breakthrough and Fontaine is again showing his eagerness, going close from a corner.

Then when Inverness seem to temporarily run out of gunpowder to launch any more of ye olde fiery spheres, Hibs hit them with two goals in the space of five minutes at the end of the first half and it's Stokes who gets them. The first comes from a cross by the ever-willing Lewis Stevenson and is down to Stokes' fox-in-the-box snideyness, as he takes a crucial step backwards to collect the ball in his midriff, leaving Josh Meekings and Gary Warren in the Caley-Thistle defence looking like tumshies, then casually swings his right foot to find the corner of the net. An easy finish, for him, and the second is even more straightforward after a Liam Henderson surge sets up Cummings for a shot which is parried by goalkeeper Owain Fon Williams right into Stokes' path and he pops the ball into the net. You could almost call this goal a stunning example of the brilliantly dovetailing Jayse-Stokesy strike partnership's intuitive appreciation of each other's style, movement and *Mr & Mrs*-grade secrets. Yes, that's exactly what it is.

Suddenly the Tulloch Caledonian doesn't seem so cold anymore, or quite so utilitarian and similar to every other ground built in the last twenty years. And it's really not. The main stand is a riot of advertising, a brashness that makes you think of the more chaotic corners of Spain or anywhere in Argentina, places just slightly warmer than Inverness.

Then there are the sea views with the Kessock Bridge climbing into the clouds. Few clubs can match this vista although given the option of having an enclosed ground I'd probably prefer that. Okay, the outlook might be restricted but wouldn't the place feel more permanent, as opposed to something easily disassembled, strapped onto four wide-load lorries and, one fateful day, carted off?

It's the kids I feel sorry for in this pop-up seat world of self-contained stands, denied the chance to wander right round the stadium. At half-time, before fan segregation, the swapping of ends was one of the great set-piece rituals. Moving off at the same moment, the rival groups would come face to face at halfway. Scarves knotted round wrists, they'd sneer at each other but there was rarely any bovver. At Easter Road the girls in the Hibee contingent were in any case more intent on grabbing the prime vantage points for Peter Marinello's dribbles down the wing. 'They call him Marinello,' the lassies sang, to the tune of Donovan's 'Mellow Yellow'. Truly this procession of his fanclub, glammed up for the afternoon, was a thrilling one for a plooky adolescent boy but these fierce C&A-clad beauties were only interested in ogling Marinello's arse, before he disappeared off to Arsenal, a once-only gig as a *Top of the Pops* presenter, an underpants modelling contract and obscurity.

*

This is not how the replay is supposed to pan out. Battered and bruised and Hampden-hungover, Hibs were expected to offer up meek surrender to Meekings & Co. But, Hibs being Hibs, there's a twist. An incredible one.

Inverness storm back into the tie after the break and Carl Tremarco has an astonishing miss, scooping the ball over the bar when it seems easier to score. Hibs drop too deep and are extremely grateful when Bartley bursts out of defence, toppling a couple of ICT gargantuans, on a fifty-yard run. But there aren't enough respites like this and Inverness eventually get a goal back when a tiring defence allow a Richie Foran knock-back to travel all the way across the six-yard box to Iain Vigurs at the near post. There were fifteen minutes remaining with Mark Oxley especially keen on a wee lie down.

Suddenly the goalie is sat on the turf, not moving, apparently sulking. After waving to the bench for assistance, seemingly because of a problem with his vision, he's failed to convince referee Stephen Finnie that another hold-up is required. This is now officially a great Scottish football contact-lens drama, although Rangers' Willie Henderson losing one of these tiny slithers of visual enhancement during an Old Firm derby and it being found, rather than trampled into the mud, by his Celtic foe Tommy Gemmell, will always rate as the best of them. Unlike Henderson, Oxley's jeepers-peepers incident doesn't have a happy ending. Hibs are winning the tie, but only just. The Inverness worthies reckon Oxley is time-wasting and roar their discontent and the official books the keeper.

Is Oxley engaged in an experiment to bend time? He's too young to remember *The Magic Boomerang*, a 1960s kids' TV import from Australia where time was actually stopped. Just one throw of a mystical curvy stick in the outback and bad guys – cattle rustlers and the like – were frozen in their tracks.

So maybe he's a frustrated illusionist, a wannabe David Copperfield, both of them having eerily well-sculpted facial hair. The Hibs fans don't like The Ox's time-tampering trick, and scream and shout at him to hurry up, because this routine never ends well. First, the opposition will go radge. The referee will add more time at the end than seems fair. The opposition will crank up their efforts and that's what happens here, but Liam Hughes' ballooned shot rivals Tremarco's for preposterousness.

Oxley tried the trick against Hearts in the previous round and was yellow-carded. Now this booking means he's out of the semi-final should Hibs get there. Like a magic-hating judge on a TV talent show Alan Stubbs slams his buzzer and Oxley is out of this game too. His replacement is a young Finn called Otso Virtanen who's never played for the first team before.

This shows right away. With the fog getting thicker Inverness wind up the catapult again and Virtanen flaps at the soaring, booming cross. It seems inevitable Hibs will concede another goal but it also seems pretty certain they'll score again. The seven minutes of stoppage time are excruciating and zany. The chances scorned by both teams are extravagant and far-fetched. Stokes blows the opportunity of a hat-trick, Henderson and Cummings should kill the tie but don't and amazingly it doesn't finish 6-4 to Hibs. Then at last it's over. What bruising affairs these last two games have been. A double-header against the Highland battalions with their iron thighs and bold ambition. Thundering conclusions but different verdicts. The Hibbies who've made this long trip are exhausted, emotional and exhilarated.

What made them come? A cold assessment of this cold night's prospects would not have been favourable. But fans think with the heart, request the afternoon off work and get on the bus, even Hibs fans, even in the Scottish Cup. They wrap up warm, shroud their hopes and dreams in their sturdiest semmits.

*

'In the lands of the North, where the Black Rocks stand guard against the cold sea, in the dark night that is very long, the Men of the Northlands sit by their great log fires and they tell a tale.'

That was how every Noggin the Nog yarn began and the little hero would have been proud of this stirring victory. Considering the lead-up and that horrible outcome at Hampden, this goes down as one of the best results of the Scottish season by any team. A performance of character no little bravery is taking Hibs back to the national stadium. But who's going to play in goal?

EIGHTEEN

'"HIBSING IT" WAS AN ATTEMPT TO DEGRADE OUR PLAYERS AND I WASN'T HAVING THAT.'

THIS, SURELY, IS where managers earn their money. Lifting a team after a mistake in the last minute has lost them a cup final so that a season of high promise isn't snuffed out completely in an inhospitable place.

'That was the first time we spoke about the Scottish Cup, about getting to the final,' says Alan Stubbs of the eve of the Inverness replay. 'We'd just lost the League Cup and we were glad to have another game so soon because we wanted to get the defeat out of our system. We had an overnight stay, which was great as the guys always got on brilliantly as a group and were all a pleasure to coach. That was our chance to re-state something: Hibs were going to make a good contribution to the season. We all believed we could. The next available opportunity was to beat Inverness and get back to Hampden. We'd just lost a final; we wanted a shot at another one.'

So what, then, did Stubbs think of the campaign to have 'Hibsing it' given full dictionary status? 'At first I thought it was a load of nonsense. Then more and more I was getting asked: "Have you Hibsed it again? Why does your club always Hibs it? Did I accept there was no known cure for Hibsing it?" Any defeat, whatever the circumstances, was being used to seriously question the players. I thought it was an attempt to degrade them and I wasn't having it.'

On the morning of the replay *The Sun* ran a story headlined 'Match of the wordplay – Jambos' dictionary dig at Hibs flops' which claimed that signatures on a petition to the *Oxford English Dictionary* had increased to 2,000 following Hibs' League Cup final defeat.

'I was working with those guys every day so I knew about their character,' adds Stubbs. '"Hibsed it" meant they'd bottled it. To question someone's bottle . . . if the people doing that had to go out and play in front of 50,000 I think the queue for the loos would be rather long.

'We were unlucky to lose to Ross County. It was a pretty even game and I knew we'd have most of the ball but that they had players who could hurt us on the counter-attack. It was similar to the Falkirk semi-final [the previous season's Scottish Cup] when we'd played well, played the best, but didn't win. That happens in football sometimes.

'There were two moments in the game, two mistakes which cost us. But their winning goal wasn't Liam Fontaine's fault; it was our fault. He was pretty cut up about it, though, and publicly apologised, which tells you about the man he is. And then he went out against Inverness and performed brilliantly which tells you about the player he is.'

Stubbs agrees that Hibs' victory in the replay against ICT took many by surprise; even if you didn't support the 'Hibsing it' petition you might still have doubted they'd be able to summon up the requisite steel, mental and physical. The manager, though, was never worried about this. 'We were in control, scored two goals which were maybe opportunistic and not like us, but then suddenly we didn't deal with a cross and rode our luck towards the end, although we also had chances to kill the game.

'It was a huge win in our season and it only reinforced what I already knew about my players: that if I had to go into battle tomorrow I'd want then behind me.' Did the slur of 'Hibsing it' drive the team on that night and for the rest of the season? 'I think it did. We spoke about the reverse psychology. I told them that there was nothing better, in any walk of life but certainly that of a footballer, than proving people wrong. Don't let anyone question what you're about, I said to them. Don't let them question who you are. We wanted to draw a line in the sand.'

NINETEEN

'I TOLD THEM THEY WERE GOING IN THE SEA IF THEY DIDN'T CLEAR OFF"

JOHN OGILVIE, WHO might be Hibs' oldest-surviving Scottish Cup warrior, is just back from his summer holidays in Corfu where, unfortunately, he had a slight accident after slipping on the tiled floor of his apartment. 'So there was no dancing for me and the wife this time,' he says with a laugh.

My reaction is to wonder about the state of the tiled floor. By the sound of it, when opponents were tackled by Oggy they tended to stay tackled. His conversation is peppered with unfortunate incidents where a winger ended up in a heap, on the cinder perimeter track or the other side of the wall.

Such as: 'We were playing Airdrie – a right good team by the way – and they had a wee lad at outside-right. I didn't mean to hurt him but we both ran at a fast pace and we clashed. He hit the boards and dropped down. I picked him right up.'

No one is left from Hibs' cup final team of 1947 but Ogilvie, having joined the previous year, watched from the Hampden stand as the Hibees lost to Aberdeen and he would go on to play a key role in a charge to the semi-finals four years later, which ended when he was the one who came a cropper.

Now eighty-six, Oggy lives with his wife Doreen in the Leicestershire town of Wigston where there's a museum dedicated to the stocking frame knitting machine and *Monty Python* funnyman Graham

Chapman was once counted among the notable inhabitants. Like footage of that long-ago era, his memory flickers and judders, until mention of a name or a game will prompt a rumbustious anecdote, raspingly delivered.

'The bloke once said to me: "You'll no' be seeing me but I'm the right winger today." "Thanks for the tip-off," I said, "and you'll be going through the gate." I can't remember his name but I didn't look to hurt anyone: the game's the game. I was sorry for the folk who got hurt, but I got hurt, too.'

Motherwell-born Ogilvie, a joiner to trade, made his Hibs debut on Christmas Day, 1948 against Queen of the South. His next match was a fourth-round tie in the Scottish Cup at home to East Fife which, despite having the full Famous Five compliment by then, the Hibees lost. 'Gordon [Smith], [Eddie] Turnbull and the rest were sorry to lose that final and all the ties after that. The cup was the one they wanted,' says Oggy.

'I was a fighter,' he continues. And a singer and a comedian and a highly sociable fellow. 'I liked the wee man [Willie Ormond] and would go and stay with him in Musselburgh when the fishing boat was out. There was a rare big pub down there. I visited Bobby [Johnstone] in Selkirk and his uncle would catch us a beautiful trout. Then Eddie invited me up to Aberdeen and we went to the dancing but he got into a spot of bother with these two guys. I told them they were going in the sea if they didn't clear off.'

Sometimes moved up to left-half, Ogilvie remembers one of the club's many friendlies against Tottenham Hotspur down in London when he scored two goals. 'There were 300 Scottish soldiers at the game. They hoisted me shoulder-high.' Straight after that Hibs went on one of their blockbusting tours, entertaining 'the continentals'. Oggy recalls a dramatic night in Germany, the opposition forgotten: 'There was this clicking sound coming from the stand. It was sten-guns. [Jock] Govan shouted at me: "Catch that one!" "Which one?"

"The one with the bloody headband!" This guy was big, 6ft 2ins, but down he went. Then we played some Russians and I knocked one of their men right over a dyke.'

In 1951 Hibs were crowned champions of Scotland for a second time but they might have won more that season, Motherwell beating them 3-0 in the League Cup final. 'The week before we'd gone to Fir Park in the league and won 6-2. Can you believe that? Gordon was brilliant that day. Afterwards I took the team to a pub. I told them: "Don't hit that guy because he's a world champion – but you'll get a drink for free."' The boxer was Dave Charnley, the Dartford Destroyer, whose parents hailed from Craigneuk.

Rangers were the danger in the Scottish Cup but in the second round at Ibrox Hibs beat them (att: the amazing 102,342). 'You can write the Hibernian victory as the greatest of their career,' wrote Alec Young of the *Edinburgh Evening News*, after they'd twice come from behind to win through Johnstone. 'I was up against the big flying-machine. You know him: Willie Waddell,' says Ogilvie. 'Willie lived two miles from me in Overton but that day I stopped him.

'Afterwards the Rangers fellas said: "John, you'll get a bloody fortune in your wages after that display." "I don't think so," I said. Waddell said: "I thought you were coming to the Rangers, you wee midden."

'Then at the old Ibrox railway station the Rangers fans were all grumbling: "That's him! He stopped Waddell!" This 6ft 3ins red-haired guy who cut big trees for houses in the yard where I was an apprentice went: "One more word and I'll throw the lot of you on the line!"'

In the quarter-finals Hibs won handsomely at Airdrie, setting up another clash with Motherwell at Tynecastle, but in a mudbath they were to lose Oggy within fifteen minutes with a double fracture of the right leg. With no substitutes in those days the Hibees fell 3-1 behind. Showing what the *Evening News* called 'terrific courage', they pulled one back and were devastated when Smith thought he'd equalised only for the goal to be disallowed.

Ogilvie missed all of the drama having been carted off to hospital and the road to recovery would be a long one. He trained with Hamilton Accies close to his home. 'They tied a ball to the roof of the gym but I could outjump the whole team. One of them played for England – big idiot!'

At Easter Road sessions he was soon back to outrunning everyone. 'No one was faster. [Lawrie] Reilly would get five yards of a start but I'd leave them all for dead. Then we'd go down to the salt-water baths at Portobello where Mick Gallagher – marine commando, nice guy – would entertain us by diving off the top board and afterwards Gordon would fling open the door of his fancy car: 'Jump in, Oggy!''

As he watched this great team continue to flop at knockout football, Ogilvie would only manage one more game for the first XI, three years after his injury. He moved on to Leicester City and in 1957 helped a Scots-dominated side win the old Second Division. 'But the Scottish Cup,' he reiterates, 'the Hibees were so desperate to win it.'

TWENTY

'GO OUT THERE AND GIE THEM "THE REEL O' TULLOCH"'

BECAUSE I WAS only one year old at the time of the 1958 final – alive, but blissfully ignorant of the latest in a series of thundering disappointments which would come to dominate my life – I'd like to know more about the defeat reckoned by many to have been Hibs' best chance of winning the cup in the last 114 years.

John Fraser was the young right-winger and the man with possibly the toughest job in Scottish football at that time – understudy for Gordon Smith – who was only going to get a game when that dreadful thing happened and the god-like genius was injured.

Today he's a dapper man of eighty living down the Forth in Joppa where he's a champion bowler. When I mention the defeat by Clyde he shakes his head. 'We were overconfident, that was our problem,' he says.

Fraser was summoned to the team after Smith had been 'chopped down once too often'. He played every game of the run to the final, scoring in the fourth-round win over Third Lanark although the goal has been relegated in the memory by a gruesome clash with Thirds' fine keeper Jocky Robertson. 'It was a 50-50 ball but I'm afraid I went right in on top of him, my studs going straight through his knee – a horrible moment. But Jocky got patched up and played on – he was a brave wee guy.'

Fraser netted the winner in the replayed semi against Rangers. 'Eric Caldow, their left-back, tried to clear the ball from the goalmouth, it hit me on the face and fair flew into the net. I can't claim much any of the credit for that being a classic goal. But we thought that by beating Rangers we'd done all the hard work and that Clyde would be straightforward.'

Playing 275 games for Hibs over the fourteen years he was at the club, Fraser says it's 'the biggest mystery surrounding Easter Road' that the Famous Five never lifted the cup. This hasn't dimmed his appreciation of their heavenly talents. 'I thought Gordon was an Adonis and how could you mind being kept out of the team by such a class act? He was a gentleman, a pleasure to know and so different to the rest of the Five: Eddie liked a drink, wee Bobby liked a drink, Lawrie was teetotal and Willie was a joker.

'Willie's party-piece – and he could still do it in '58 – was to skip along the byline and shoot from an impossible angle. Keepers mind the near post now but nine times out of ten Willie scored. And Eddie, even though he'd moved to right-half was still driving us on. He played behind me and would take the throw-ins. If I didn't return the ball to him correctly the flames would shoot down his nostrils.'

Fraser got around by pig van. His father-in-law owned a smallholding and Fraser would collect the leftovers from notable Edinburgh addresses like St Andrew's House, the Scottish Office HQ, which were then turned into pigfeed. The young Pat Stanton was ferried to training in the van and Joe Baker hitched a pungent ride to the North British Hotel to sign for Torino. He returned to the van with a bulging cloth bag. 'What's in it?' asked Fraser. 'My signing-on fee,' replied Baker.

Baker's departure was a loss for the cup dreamers – 'Joe was so quick: in the head and over ten yards,' says Fraser, who continued the quest for the trophy in places like Brechin, venue for a much-postponed tie in the ferocious winter of 1963. He scored that afternoon after dodging the sharp spikes of a rotovator parked dangerously close to the pitch – just another cup hazard to be confronted by the Hibees.

Then Willie Hamilton joined the club, seeming to possess the elusive talent which could net the elusive trophy, although Jock Stein when he took charge of Hibs a few months later wasn't impressed by the player's application, which was similarly elusive.

'It's not a nice thing to say about someone who's no longer with us but Willie was always turning up hungover,' recalls Fraser. 'I was captain so I got summoned to Jock's office where he told me: 'I'm going to humiliate Willie Hamilton in front of everyone.' After training Jock said to him: 'You're a disgrace to yourself and to Hibernian Football Club. Collect your clothes and get out – and don't come back until I call for you.' Three weeks later he returned transformed. You know, Willie was intelligent. I remember the director Alex Pratt picking up a copy of *The Scotsman* on the team-bus with the crossword completed and asking: "Who's the brainbox?" It was Willie. He was a magician with a football and a lovely man but sometimes an awfie one.' He couldn't win Hibs the cup either, despite choreographing a run to the semi-finals in 1965. 'Willie had been brilliant for us, especially in beating Rangers in the quarters when he scored, but just before we played Dunfermline Jock called me into his office again. 'It's been my life's ambition to manage Celtic,' he said. I said: 'You'll be waiting until the end of the season, won't you?' But he left right away. We were devastated.'

After hanging up his boots Fraser joined Turnbull's coaching staff for what would be Hibs' only other final appearances of the twentieth century, in 1972 and 1979. Turnbull was an inspirational manager but unwilling to indulge his players. 'It's a cliché, I know, but sometimes footballers need an arm round the shoulder. Eddie hated doing that.' Turnbull was just as reluctant to deviate from an all-out attacking philosophy. 'Hibs should have won the European Cup-Winners' Cup in 1973. Leading 4-2 against Hajduk Split going to Yugoslavia I suggested putting John Blackley behind two centre-halves and holding onto our lead. The flames came down the nostrils again. 'There's no effing chance of me doing that,' he said. Eddie was a purist. He wanted footballers on the park, no brutes allowed. You had to be able to play to be in his team.'

Fraser reflects again on '58 and while Baker – 'A happy-go-lucky nice guy' – was Hibs' likeliest match-winner, Andy Aitken was key to their hopes. 'But Clyde had done their homework on Andy and crocked him in the first ten minutes. He really made us tick, buzzing all over the place – a bit like John McGinn does for Hibs now – and that was a huge blow.

'We thought we could win the cup that day. We weren't coached – that didn't really happen back then. We had a trainer, Jimmy McColl, while Hugh Shaw, the manager, stayed in the office. The only time we saw Hugh between games was on the Monday if we'd had a bad result on the Saturday. He'd put on his bunnet and hammer us round the track and up the terracing – it was punishment.

'Before the final he said to us: "Right lads, I want you to go out there and gie them 'The Reel o' Tulloch'." Hugh was a Highlander who could play the bagpipes, but the precise meaning of that instruction was lost on us, I'm afraid.

'The fans were so disappointed that day. They'd given the players brilliant encouragement but then they really did see the best football around – Hibs in the 1950s were a right bonnie team. We used to have our pre-match meal in the Scotia Hotel in Edinburgh's New Town then travel in taxis to home games. By 2.00 o'clock the supporters would be queueing right to the top of Easter Road. In '58 they thought we were going to bring home the cup and so did we. It was going to take them a long, long time to get over that one.'

*

But Willie didn't bend the plate. A notorious tale seemingly emblematic of Hibs' carelessness with silverware concerns a salver awarded to Hamilton on the 1965 summer tour of Canada. Peter Cormack once told me that when Hammy realised the dish wouldn't fit in his bag he casually folded it in half. Fraser, though, roomed with Hamilton on that trek, was sharing a taxi with the player when they learned of the prize for a man-of-the-match display, shouted in vain for the ball against Ottawa All-Stars as the wayward wizard kept it to himself while scoring seven of Hibs' 15 goals – 'and yes it's a wonderful, daft story which sums up a wonderful, daft player but I don't think he was actually going to bend the plate. He placed it over his knee and I said, "Willie, don't!" He just laughed.'

TWENTY-ONE

'SEE YOU AT THE WEE BARRIER'

16 April 2016
Hibernian 0 Dundee United 0
(Hibernian win 4-2 on penalties)

YOU NEVER FORGET your first time. My big Hampden debut was the Scottish Cup semi-final of 1972, on a sparkling spring day suddenly turned apocalyptic by a giant red dust-cloud. Hundreds of Rangers fans had converged on the stadium's slopes at exactly the same time. Claiming their places at the end they called, with a keen sense of privilege, the 'Rangers End', they'd kicked up the ash which in those days formed the terrace steps. Some might have been wearing Doc Marten boots but this was a BBC nuclear drama-type dust-cloud, suggestive of a much sharper heel. It wouldn't have been a surprise if many among the Ibrox legions had got dressed up for the occasion in Freeman, Hardy & Willis' finest stack-heeled boots. This was semi-final day, after all, when their team would have been expected to win.

They didn't win that day, Hibs coming back to grab a draw and in the replay played Rangers off the park. I'd never seen Hibs beat Rangers before, and was astonished this was allowed. For the final, Hibs fans were moved to the surprisingly available Rangers End, while the rival Celtic supporters took their usual places in the – wait for it – Celtic End. Clearly Hibs had a bit to go to break the duopoly but if your team hadn't won the cup for seventy years as it was then, you could hardly claim proprietorial rights in the ground. And it would be seventy-one years at least: Celtic romped to a 6-1 victory and an exceedingly spherical striker called Dixie Deans scored a hat-trick.

The match programme acknowledged Hibs as a coming team but drooled over Jock Stein's men: 'Abroad, they catch their breath, the continental experts, and tell you: "Ah, Celtic are so fast, so unusual in attack, so strong!"'

Deans might have looked unusual but he wasn't. The non-sylph-like, as-wide-as-he-is-tall footballer was quite common back then. Every team had one and indeed Celtic had two – Dixie and 'Fat' Pat McCluskey. But they were effective, especially Deans, who was a holy terror when rolled out against Hibs, bagging two further hat-tricks against them in 1974 in the space of a week. The one in the '72 brought him most joy, though, as evidenced by his attempt at a somersault celebration. We all knew, and loved, Olga Korbut, but this was Olga Doughnut. It was a hilarious, touching moment in Hampden history and one – thanks to better diet and conditioning and the greater athletic demands of the sport – we were never going to witness again.

*

But hang on: we've just spotted our goalie for today. Conrad Logan is big. Not dumpy like Dixie and with his extra height he should be able to carry that build better and he does, kind of, but these are definitely moobs he's flaunting. In the evolution of man and the changes to body shape since the glam-rock era, man-breasts didn't exist forty-four years ago, or if they did they were kept well hidden. Dean's strip was baggier and he wisely decided against finishing off his improbable gymnastics floor-routine by removing it.

Poor Logan doesn't have the advantage of concealment; he's got to go with shirt fashion, which is shiny and tight. Managers are required to wear shiny and tight suits on the touchline, all of them following the style leader, Pep Guardiola, and trying not split their breeks as has happened twice to novice coach Zinedine Zidane. Referees are only too happy to wear shiny and tight tunics as they seek to create celebrity status for themselves. Players have been shiny and tight for a while.

In his shrieking green top, Logan fields shots in a training goal and the entire Hibs support studies the team warm-up like never before. No one has clapped eyes on the blond-haired, ruddy-cheeked Irishman before; all we know is that he's 'come from Leicester City', admittedly supreme credentials right now, given that the Foxes are threatening the greatest-ever title triumph in English football history. But none of us knew until this minute that he'd be playing. Anxious conversations create an unusual pre-match hum. Many of them begin 'What the . . . ?' or 'Have you seen . . . ?'

To replace the suspended Mark Oxley the choice for Alan Stubbs was the young, nervous Finn, Otso Virtanen, or the former Leicester stand-in, largely unused by them for ten seasons, who's been just about everywhere on loan including Scunthrope twice, but who hasn't played a first-team game since 2014.

The fans are apprehensive; how ready for a semi-final debut can he be? Stubbs had better be sure. But does Logan look worried, or self-conscious about the fact that half the stadium is scrutinising him in mild disbelief? Not really, and then he lollops back to the dressing-room for final instructions, and maybe to conduct a last namecheck of his newest team-mates.

*

Hampden today is a drastically slimmed-down version of its old self. It's as if a giant egg-slicer removed the top half and the most interesting bits. These included the old press-box, perched precariously on the roof of the main stand and seeming to offer a rear-gunner's view of the world, and the high, slim shelf of a stand across the pitch. And the wee barrier, that's gone too.

'See you at the wee barrier,' chirruped one imp to his mate outside the great bowl in '72. Even Celtic's urchin fans had a confidence about them, my father and I spotting these two splitting up to join different queues, increasing their chances of a 'lift-over'. We didn't expect to see them again, not in a crowd which would rise to 106,101, but ended up next to a stanchion which was indeed wee, and after two hours when one them was perched on it, anxiously scanning the throng, the pals were happily reunited just before kick-off.

Meanwhile there was me, stuck to my dad's side, fifteen years old but not yet ready for the boldness and robustness of these much younger boys, and in tears by the time Celtic's sixth rippled the net.

*

Hibs will have to be strong today. They lost the League Cup final here just a few weeks before and in the Championship a run of one win from eight has killed their chances of the title. Bound for the playoffs, they're not even in second spot anymore, Falkirk staying ahead of them when the teams met four nights ago, wiping out a two-goal lead in the last three minutes to snatch an audacious draw. The 'Hibsing it' lobby loved that.

But Dundee United's form is even worse. They're bottom of the Premiership which represents a sad decline for a club who were once the most vibrant in the country. Roared on by their mad-genius manager Jim McLean, they won the 1982-83 title using just fourteen players, many of them like Paul Sturrock and David Narey irresistibly modern. Famous wins over Manchester United and Barcelona allowed newspaper sub-editors to show off their knowledge of krautrock, inspiring the headline 'Tangerine Dream'. Only cheating Roma prevented the club from reaching the European Cup final.

Now United seem doomed. Of course, they could transform themselves from league slugs into cup butterflies; that happens sometimes when the pressure is off. They hold a decisive lead over Hibs in the tournament head-to-head and have won the last four ties. The first chance falls to them and Billy McKay, not so long ago Scottish football's hottest shot, would have fancied himself one-on-one with the keeper but hadn't reckoned on that being Logan. None of us had, and the man from Donegal makes himself big, or bigger, to swallow him up.

United, though, are a mess at the back. In their previous game, one of their defenders picked up the ball and walked off the pitch. There's almost a repeat of the bizarre incident here, much to the annoyance of manager Mixu Paatelainen, the ex-Hibee. And then they concede a penalty.

Jason Cummings had been determined to have a better Hampden experience than last time when the League Cup final seemed to overwhelm him. After trying too hard in that game, the advice might have been: 'Keep it simple.' But that's not Cummings' way. What was really needed here, he reckoned, was to take his crazy vaudeville act to another level, to increase the wow factor. For the spot-kick he decided to try a Panenka.

Antonin Panenka astonished the football world in 1976 with his softly chipped penalty over an already committed and prostate goalkeeper to win Czechoslovakia the European Championships. Cummings' attempt doesn't do this; it clears the bar by a couple of feet. There's huge disgruntlement among the Hibs fans. United, incensed by his effrontery, race up the other end. Again McKay finds himself with a clear run on goal only to be foiled once more by Logan. As the anticipated hero of the day – according to his own script – ponders the likelihood of a bad press, a new and unlikely one might be emerging.

*

Although Hibs have had great goalies down the years – from Tommy Younger to Ronnie Simpson to Andy Goram, as well as Alan Rough and Jim Leighton in the autumn of their careers – it has been a problem position more recently. There were enough of them who dropped the ball in an Edinburgh derby – Zibi Malkowski, Simon Brown, Andy McNeil – to form a psychotherapy group. Yves Ma-Kalambay was quickly nicknamed My Calamity. Ole Gottskalksson was described by his manager as 'like a drunk trying to catch a balloon'. And Jim Herriot, the Turnbull's Tornadoes goalie who shared in all that team's best days, carried the can for one of the worst, a crushing European Cup-Winners' Cup defeat in Split, when he lost the flight of the ball under the weird Yugoslavian floodlighting, despite his usual practice of blackening his eyes with goalmouth dirt.

Of course Hibs didn't qualify for that tournament as cup *winners*. Celtic took the trophy but a more glamorous option awaited them for also winning the title. Hibs, as thrashed runners-up, stood in for them.

After the half-time break, when there must have been some lively discussion over the pro-performance Digestives about that penalty miss, Logan resumes being the semi-final's dominant character. There's a fine save from John Rankin and an even better one from Henri Anier, the third one-on-one duel where he's psyched out his opponent, standing tall and wide. This prompts a beautiful moment: applause ripples through the Hibee support, right round the half-moon East Stand, for what this burly stranger is achieving today.

He's keeping Hibs in the contest. United are not brilliant by any means but they're having the more clear-cut chances. The tiredness which caused Hibs to lose to already-relegated Alloa Athletic the week before is evident again. But so in the tenaciousness from the previous rounds against Inverness and Hearts.

As they say about semi-finals: lose them and no one remembers you. You're the Plain Janes or Speccy Sids at the end-of-year dance, liable to be swept up with the fag-butts. The Hibee saga of cup disappointment has a fat chapter dedicated to last-four losses. This is their seventh semi-final in twelve years; only Celtic with eight have appeared in more. Three years in a row they failed at this stage, the first in 2005 with a young team featuring six future Scotland internationalists and Derek Riordan, Garry O'Connor and Steven Fletcher in attack. They were winning against Dundee United but fell to two late goals. It might sound like they 'Hibsed' that one, but the phrase wasn't in use back then. Instead, if you wanted to be disparaging about that generation of Hibees when they didn't quite live up to the audacious hairstyles, you said they 'boybanded it'.

But when Hibs lost their most recent semi, last year to Falkirk in Stubbs' first season, there was a significant change. They didn't freeze on Hampden's expanse but performed well and were unfortunate. Hibs were losing differently and, if this was possible, losing better. Stubbs was getting the players to express themselves on the big occasions. The outcome was still in the lap of the dogs but there was progress.

*

Dogged is the word for this performance. Although their demanding schedule has clearly taken its toll Hibs haven't buckled. The games are catching up with the likes of John McGinn who's gone ninety minutes further than the rest having won his first Scotland cap in a friendly against Denmark when he was voted man-of-the-match. But while nothing like scintillating, the team have hung in there.

The semi goes to extra-time, two knackered sides scrapping to a complete standstill. The fans are drained, too. Semis take you to the window of the toyshop and that can be your lot. One goal would have settled this. If it had gone to United, the taunts about the curse extending by one more year would have begun on the final whistle.

Now penalties will decide a game which has already featured surely the most idiotic spot-kick Hampden has ever seen. United go first, Blair Spittal setting down the ball. Logan, bouncing and jiggling, seems to be shouting at the player, goading him. Spittal starts his run-up and Logan is still yelling. The United man is so freaked by the rant that all he can do is hit it straight at the mad Irishman. Logan saves.

McGinn nets Hibs' first penalty and then McKay steps up. Same routine from Logan; same outcome. In celebration he turns to the Hibs fans and roars himself purple. Scarcely believing his blarney and bluster, they roar right back. The Hibees keep slotting their penalties – Paul Hanlon and Martin Boyle, both excellent – until they have the chance to win the tie. Who else but Cummings steps forward from the halfway-line huddle. What will happen this time? He goes low and not really that hard but scores. Hibs are through to another final, having beaten a Premiership team for the sixth time this season, and in the euphoria Stubbs doesn't forget that one team had just lost in the cruellest manner and commiserates with the United players.

Cummings runs to the stands to take the acclaim, the star of his own self-produced reality show yet again. But his teammates rush straight for Logan standing on the other side of the goal and swamp him. Cummings to be fair to him then heads straight over there himself.

Post-match, the gallus lad seems to think a question about a penalty refers to the one that counted and not the one that hopelessly didn't. Cummings explains that the inspiration for his Panenka was a combination of Italy's Andrea Pirlo, who successfully dinked England from the spot, and his latest haircut, the latter presumably having its own Twitter account already. This is the story of the afternoon for, oh, all of eight seconds because now Logan is talking about his incredibly roundabout journey to a Scottish Cup semi-final, how he was grateful to Stubbs for showing faith in him when he wondered where his next gig was coming from, how he commiserated with Virtanen for being picked ahead of his young rival – and how his nickname is the Polar Bear.

But I wouldn't be too hard on Cummings. He's got the ballsiness that everyone says Hibs lack on big match days. His trick-shot didn't work but come the shoot-out he didn't hide. He was smiling as he left his teammates in the middle of the park and it wasn't so much a walk to the penalty-spot as a strut. He turned round to his pals and laughed, doubtless at their warnings not to blow it this time. He was beaming like mad when he collected the ball from the previous United kick-taker. Who else behaves like this in Scottish football? Are we not always moaning about the lack of characters?

Cummings is grateful to Logan for sparing his blushes, or as close as he ever gets to self-consciousness, and we're grateful to have another chance to break the hoodoo. At least I think we are.

Fans of other Scottish clubs don't like Hampden since its redevelopment. Maybe they're there too often or not at all. Hibs get to the stadium pretty regularly but are never successful, so for them it takes on a different aspect. It's gruesome and yet fascinating, like the haunted house on the hill in children's fiction or the S&M nightclub down the dingy alley. It's a necessary evil if your team are going to lift the Scottish Cup one day.

Hampden is where I've been my happiest as a fan – not in the Scottish Cup, obviously, but the three League Cups Hibs have won – and where I've been my saddest. That 6-1 defeat in 1972 was tough to take. What I didn't know was that the Scottish Cup for the Hibees was going to progress from sad to bad to diabolical.

Hampden is where I've been my most humiliated and where I was nine years ago, scared as hell and excited as hell, and wondering how my extremely pregnant wife was faring fifty miles away and whether I might get the call over the public-address to rush back in time to begin fatherhood.

Our antenatal class were appalled I was going to that year's League

Cup final to risk missing the birth. I mean, I remember when the bigger concern confronting a father-to-be was about missing the football. My father was fond of intoning a crackly Tannoy announcement mid-match from the era of Unreconstructed Scottish Fitba Man: 'Shuggie McGonagall – when you eventually get home tonight you'll be meeting the triplets. Important info regarding the size of the carryout you'll need from Agnews: they're all girls. Nae luck pal.' Dad was exaggerating for comic effect, but not by much.

I wanted to hear my name called. Of course I would have been absolutely wetting myself if I had been required to belt back over Harthill in the freakish whiteout that day, but a perverse part of me wanted to appal the baby-group some more because these are people who will never know what it feels like to throw open the curtains on the morning of a final – and particularly the morning of a Scottish Cup final – and scream silently to yourself: 'Crikey, what's going to happen *today*?'

'YOU REACH A MOMENT WHEN YOU START TO THINK THINGS MIGHT BE HAPPENING FOR A REASON'

WHAT IF HIBS had been promoted the previous season? What if Alan Stubbs had been lured away? What if Scott Allan had stayed? What if John McGinn hadn't arrived? Or that bubbletastic bottle of extra-fizzy pop Liam Henderson? Would they still have won the Scottish Cup? These are the questions Hibbies occasionally ask themselves, because many of them remain fatalists. And here's another one: what if Mark Oxley hadn't lost a contact lens in the Invernessian glaur because, bless him, some goalies never look like they're ever going to save a penalty?

'The decision to try and find another keeper was taken on the bus back down from Inverness,' says Stubbs. 'Mark was out of the semi-final and Otso [Virtanen] didn't get the confidence from the few minutes he was on the park that we would have liked for his sake. We thought the semi might be too much for him.

'We asked Graeme Mathie, our head of recruitment, to see what was available. I knew Conrad Logan's name but I didn't know he'd been out of action for so long. I've got to say that when I saw the shape of him I was . . . surprised. But right away in training he was good. From having been just in the door two minutes, he was vocal, commanding, infectious, though obviously he was carrying a little extra weight.

'We were thinking: can he cope with those additional pounds? Will he be agile enough to get across the goal? We were limited to what keepers were available. Other targets hadn't materialised. But a week later Conrad was still impressing us. Yes, he looked like a footballer from the 1970s. But his issues didn't seem to be a burden on his ability to keep a ball out of the back of the net.'

Stubbs didn't witness Jason Cummings' attempted Panenka. 'I never look at penalties and at that moment I nipped to the loo. I knew he'd missed and found out when I got back that he tried a chip. It was obviously a chance for us to lead after starting well, but then Dundee United came into the game and Conrad made his great blocks. At half-time I didn't say to Jason: "What the effing hell were you trying to do?" I was like, all right, it happened, now let's try and win this game. I saw his Panenka later. Did I want to strangle him after that? Yeah.'

As the two teams slugged it out through extra-time Stubbs watched exhausted players who'd given everything in a punishing sequence of matches. 'I knew I needed to rest some of them but because of the magnitude of the games I couldn't quite do it. With hindsight I should have done.' During the shootout he looked towards the Hibs end hoping for a good reaction. 'Conrad used all his experience there. Shootouts are battles of wits and a lot of goalies beat themselves by going too early. He waited for a split-second longer each time.'

The lost lens, the suspension, other goalies not coming to Hibs' aid, then an out-of-condition penalty specialist answering the call . . . was everything about the semi-final victory down to fate? 'Well, you maybe reach a moment when you start to think things might be happening for a reason. Regarding Hibs and the cup, it was hard not to wonder if everything wasn't already mapped out. But in view of the club's history you'd have a hard job convincing those poor, long-suffering fans that we were predestined to win it.'

Does he think his cancer was mapped out? 'Maybe, who knows?

I got picked for a random drug test after a game which detected it. Maybe, if a problem had developed later, I'd have been a typical man and not got it checked out. And if someone else had been chosen for that test instead I probably wouldn't be here talking to you about winning the Scottish Cup – that's the utter coldness of this.'

Stubbs' lack of animation as a manager, almost to the point of invisibility, is fascinating in an age when technical areas have been a battleground of eye-jabbing, tie-yanking, c-word abuse and headbutting of passing players – and rarely less than a frenzy of air marshal arm-waving. But then remember his father, watching over his boyhood kickabouts from the wall at Windy Harbour, was 'dead understated'.

'A manager's work is done Monday to Friday. There's not much that can be changed on matchdays. A lot of the jumping around you see is done for effect. If a manager is waving his arms about and hurling insults does he really that's going to make a player perform better?'

These days, says Stubbs, there are plenty of winning managers who are the personification of calm. 'I'm not saying I'm one of them,' he adds, but we shouldn't regard his quiet detachedness, or his post-cancer attitude that football is not the matter of life and death he once believed it to be, as evidence of a lack of ambition. 'My desire for success is probably greater than when I was a player. As a player I felt in control of my own destiny. Now I'm a manager I feel more vulnerable because eighteen to twenty-four other guys are in charge of that destiny. But ultimately the satisfaction when things go well is greater.'

Post-cancer, Stubbs strives to banish negativity from his life. 'I always try to be positive although sometimes that's easier said than done.' Well, that upbeat half-time message to Cummings might have helped the player who ultimately scored the winning penalty. And when assessing Logan's chances of becoming a potential Hibee hero the manager ignored the minuses and went with the pluses. The big Irishman will never have to buy a drink in Leith again.

TWENTY-THREE

'THE ALDERSHOT FANS WERE SINGING "YOU'RE JUST A FAT PETER SCHMEICHEL"'

ONCE THROUGH THE doors of Spotland there are two windows, one for Rochdale AFC and the other for Rochdale Hornets, the rugby league team. Equal status on the ground floor, the rugby boys seem to have more to shout about upstairs with a better-stocked trophy cabinet and blown-up photographs of the great Eddie Waring, a touring Fiji team's early 1960s visit to the Lancashire town of Gracie Fields, Cyril Smith and the clock tower Adolf Hitler was going to ship to Nazi Germany once had he won the war.

The football team's enlarged shot, on the other hand, is of the players' celebrations following a goal in an FA Cup-tie in 2003. The blue plastic seats behind them are empty. The poster records the attendance that day: 2,566.

In a modest town – with stair-rod rain greeting today's Feel Good Festival where the headline act are the Fratellis – this is an extremely modest football club. 'Never made it out of the lower two tiers of English football,' director David Bottomley tells me. 'We had thirty-six years in the fourth, the longest run of any of the original ninety-two clubs without any kind of success. Of the ninety-two, only Rochdale and Hartlepool have never played in the top two divisions so for the 125th anniversary of the Football League the fixtures were arranged so we could play each other on the opening day, which was an honour of sorts. But this is our third consecutive season in the third tier, our

best performance since the early 1970s. For a long time the bottom
league was nicknamed the Rochdale Division. When we finally got
out of it our fans sung: "It needs a new name, it needs a new name/
This Rochdale Division, it needs a new name."'

No longer quite the bottomleyest club in England, the director
and a faithful old retainer are arguing at reception about whether
Conrad Logan was a four-game hero for Rochdale back in 2014 or a
five-game one. This was the goalkeeper's eighth loan spell away from
parent club Leicester City but these Dale diehards are agreed: he was
brilliant for them. 'The Aldershot fans sang "You're just a fat Peter
Schmeichel,"' recalls Bottomley. Logan would save penalties in three
consecutive games and have this one-month loan extended, only then
he got injured. It was the Achilles in his right foot, a nasty one. He
wondered if he would play again. For sixteen months he didn't. Then
– and there's no disputing this – he became an eight-game hero for
Hibs.

The Polar Bear is back from training. He offers such a baby-soft
handshake that I'm wondering how he ever managed to beat away
those penalties in the semi-final shootout. He leads me into one of
the executive boxes with a panorama of sodden Spotland and we talk
about his brief, beautiful life as a Hibee which Hollywood would
surely reject as too sugary sweet.

'When I was trying to come back from the injury, which happened
right out there,' he says, 'I had to leave Leicester completely as there
was an insurance problem with me training with the players, so I was
doing a bit here and a bit there, Bury for a week, then back here and
I'd just finished a Tuesday session when there was a missed call from
my agent: did I want to go to Hibs?

'Maybe it was going to be a single-game loan. By all accounts they
just needed another keeper who could sit on the bench. I went up
and, because of an international break no one was around, so I did
some work with the youths. I didn't meet Alan Stubbs and the first

team until the following week. The gaffer said he wanted to do a deal. I thought, yeah, okay. I wasn't wanting to be a cheerleader for Hibs. If there was a chance of playing in the semi-final I wanted it. But just being part of a squad again was going to be good for me. Worst case scenario: I got just the one game. But I'd have trained for eight weeks with a club who had a lot to play for. That was a whole lot better than the place I'd just been.'

Logan, dressed in black, looks trimmer than when Hibs fans were provided with their first unforgettable glimpse of him at Hampden. His story is related with a furry Donegal burr. He has piercing blue eyes made all the more striking by his swooping blond eyebrows. He gets close to tears talking about the injury to his right foot. It left him frustrated, depressed and fearing for the future for him and his young family.

'It was the worst time in my career. I didn't have a club for eight months and the injury was such that I couldn't properly train for a year. It was sore just walking, hurting and pinching. My foot would swing out to the side because there was no power in it to push straight through. I used to have to sit with it up in the air, watching daytime TV and going a bit demented. I was regularly down in London seeing this surgeon. He told me the fastest anyone came back from a tendon injury like mine was six months but warned me it could take as long as two years. When I went well past the six months I started to panic. My partner Victoria and I have two kids, Niamh and Finn. We'd managed to scrape through with what I'd made from Leicester but I was thinking: "I can't do my job. I can't provide. Are we going to struggle?" I couldn't see where my next game of football was coming from.'

Logan's only previous visits to Edinburgh were for Christmas parties with Leicester organised by the Scottish players recruited by former manager Craig Levein. Hibs put him up in a flat in Tranent, East Lothian close to their training complex. He loved going to work again, and fitted in well with his new team-mates.

'It was a good dressing-room with good camaraderie. Sometimes young players can be quiet and they'll be in one corner and the experienced pros who've played 400 games will be in another but that wasn't the case at Hibs. Jason [Cummings] and Keats [James Keatings] were little jokers and Hendo [Liam Henderson] was another.

'Every game was important at that stage. League points were needed and the semi-final was coming. But it wasn't a tense dressing-room. I didn't think I'd walked into this haunted place although I got a surprise when I found out how long it had been since Hibs last won the cup. I remembered the club from watching Scottish football as a kid back in Donegal; they were one of the next biggest teams after the Old Firm. George Craig [head of football operations] was giving me a lift to the airport when I had the chance to nip back home to see the family. "Win the cup and you'll become a legend," he said. I thought: "Yeah, but everyone wants to win the cup, and everyone who does becomes a legend." Then he told me about the 114 years. Wow . . .'

Logan's father Joe was a clever midfielder for Sligo Rovers and Finn Harps in the League of Ireland but from the age of four growing up in the tiny town of Ramelton (pop: 1,212) young Conrad had his heart set on being a keeper. 'I saw Pat Bonner save that penalty at Italia '90 [shoot-out vs Romania, Republic of Ireland progressing to the World Cup quarter-finals] and wanted to be him. I made my granny roll up socks and throw them at me and I'd try and dive across the living-room and save them just like Packie, always with one foot up in the air.

'I never played a game of a football, not even a kickabout, in any position other than keeper. No need for the wee guy with glasses normally picked last to go in goal; the big blond fella would always do it. And I loved that I came from Goalie County. Packie was a Donegal man, as was his successor Shay Given. My dad knew Shay's dad and got me a pair of his gloves when I was twelve – green Adidas Fingersaves. I wore them until all my fingers popped right through and they were in tatters.'

One foot up in air like Packie. That's what Logan wanted to be doing again, not one foot up in the air in front of *Homes under the Hammer*, trying to drain the lactic acid – and the doubt and the worry over his Achilles. On 16 April, two days before his thirtieth birthday, he got his chance.

'I'd watched the games in the lead-up to the semi-final but hadn't been involved – Otso [Virtanen] was on the bench. There was the defeat at Alloa. Hibs would have been a scalp for them and I'd imagine a few of the teams in the Championship will have played that way and tried to drag Hibs down to their level. Then Falkirk came back from two-nil behind which was another blow but the gaffer and the players all stayed positive that week; I was really impressed by that.

'Obviously it was going to be Otso playing at Hampden or this Irish fella no one had seen before. I didn't think about [the rivalry] too much otherwise my head might have got fried. If I was the younger man I might have been going: who's the guy on the club's books with the three-year deal? Ah, but who's got the most experience? Ah, but who's also been out injured for a long time? I was thinking that if it was to be me who was picked, brilliant. If not, then making the bench for a cup semi-final was still a little step on the long road back. The gaffer told me I was playing eighty minutes before kick-off.

'I wasn't nervous; I felt great. Training had gone well and I couldn't wait to play again, albeit I didn't look my best. I wasn't self-conscious about that. No time in my career have I been small. Maybe some of the Hibs fans looking at me at the start were unsure about their new goalie, possibly one or two were worried. Not being big-headed but anywhere I've gone, and I've been lots of places, I've done a decent job. I wasn't perturbed.'

That sizeable frame blocked out the sun for Dundee United's Billy McKay, thwarted for the first of Logan's three stunning blocks during the regulation ninety minutes. He actually saved it with Packie's leg. 'Maybe my defence were thinking: "The guy hasn't played for so long, how's he going to handle this?" Maybe after I'd made some saves, one or two as a result of them being caught out, that might have changed to: "Thank God he was there."'

So what did he think of Cummings' attempt to Panenka the penalty? 'If I could have run upfield fast enough I would have clobbered him! Honestly, I picked up my water-bottle and was watching with the fifth official. When the ball drifted over the bar I looked back at the guy: "Is there going to be a re-take? Did that actually just happen?"

'When I thought some more, even though I'd only known Jason a few weeks, I wasn't surprised he tried it. He's a fantastic player who can do special things; unfortunately that one didn't come off. A lot of boys would have their head between their legs at half-time waiting for the bollocking. The gaffer to be fair said: "It's gone, maybe don't try that again, go out and score us the winner." But I did think that if we got another penalty I wouldn't have put it past Jason to try another Panenka.'

How attuned are footballers' antennae to crowd noise? Do they notice sudden changes and spontaneous sounds, such as the acclaim from the Hibs fans greeting the third of Logan's stunning, smothering blocks? 'Yeah, I heard that, it was lovely. I like one-on-ones, they're a chance for the keeper to become the hero! The pressure is all on the striker to score. I was enjoying the game and those saves. The crowd seemed to think I was doing alright.

'I didn't reckon I was unbeatable; goalies never think that. It wasn't a great game but it was, I think, a good, honest team performance from the guys that day. Everyone covered each other's backs because United had some tricky lads in the forward line. Paul [Hanlon] and Darren [McGregor] in front of me were excellent and I told Marvin Bartley afterwards that he was brilliant. I got man-of-the-match but the award should have gone to him.' So how was he looking forward to the prospect of penalty kicks? 'I was quite excited to be honest.'

There was a point in Logan's career, though, when he didn't have a good record of saving spot-kicks and he remembers his father taking him to task about this. 'He said to me: "You never stop penalties, do you?" He was right. So I set about trying to change that. At Luton Town I saved three on the way to the team winning the Johnstone's Paint Trophy. I developed little techniques.

'Realistically, the penalty-taker should score so I try to put all the pressure on him. For the first one that day I was shouting [at Blair Spittal]: "Down the middle! Down the middle!" I was trying to eliminate that option, force him to go either left or right, making it 50-50.' Maybe Spittal was brainwashed by the shouts, though, because his attempt was pretty straight.

Logan's next save was even better, a low dive to the right to send his new fan club into raptures. 'That was Billy McKay, wasn't it? I knew him at Leicester when he was a kid there and spoke to him before the game, a lovely lad. I remember taking as long as possible to return to the goal-line. I'd only just got there when he hit it. Obviously I was trying to make him nervous. He looked like he wanted to hit it quick, get rid of it. I had a feel for what he might do, maybe try to whip it, and I got it right.

'Our penalties were as good as you could hope to see anywhere. Well, maybe apart from the winning one from Jason. He was smiling and laughing as he walked up. I thought: "Everything about today will have to be Jason's way. He's going to do what he's going to do." I couldn't really watch. It wasn't the best penalty. It was slow and not in the corner and if their keeper had guessed right he'd have caught it.'

Logan was the big story and what a terrific yarn it was. He wasn't in the best shape for this crucial tie, doubtless spreading encouragement through United's fans beforehand just as anxiety went round the Hibs end. He hadn't played behind this defence before. He hadn't played any kind of game for sixteen months. He was, by his own estimation, only sixty per cent fit. And he was still carrying the effects of his injury. 'Watching the film of the game later I got a bit of a shock: as I walked to my line for the penalties I was limping.'

When the new hero returned to the dressing-room after the post-match interviews his team-mates treated him to the Ice-Bucket Challenge. 'The feeling I had afterwards was one of pride. Pride that I could still play, that I wasn't letting down my family. It had been an incredibly difficult time for Victoria and the kids and my parents. I went back out to the centre-circle to phone home, then called my father in Donegal. I bumped into Packie Bonner right after that. He said: 'Was that you calling your agent?' I told him it was Dad and he liked that because the old man had been one of Packie's favourite players.

'That call was pretty emotional. I think it lasted five minutes but neither of us really said anything. I was blubbing and Dad wasn't much more coherent. But my daughter was funny. I asked her if she enjoyed the game. "It was okay," she said, "but why didn't you save the other two penalties?" She had a point about the third one. I changed my mind at the last minute. Anyway, it all worked out grand.'

The morning after, back in Tranent, Logan was down early at his local shop to buy the papers. 'Before the semi-final I walked around the town unnoticed. That day folk were doing double-takes and pointing and shouting: "Great game, big felly!" In the shop I guessed I would be on the back of the papers so, feeling a bit self-conscious about that, I made sure they were all frontways up when I got to the counter. But the barcodes are on the back, aren't they? The shopkeeper had a laugh about that, as did everyone else in the queue. They all clapped me out of the shop.'

TWENTY-FOUR

'THE FANS WHO'VE THROWN THEIR SCARVES AWAY, WILL THEY GET THEM BACK?'

ONE OF THE phrases most used and overused by footballers – and to be fair, at the end of the day, taking each game as it comes, there are many of them – is the one which attempts to bring about a swift end to the interrogation which follows a bad defeat. 'We'll pick ourselves up, dust ourselves down and go again,' the player will say, tugging his ear nervously, before ducking out of the camera's range.

I don't know if any Hibee said these words right after the 5-1 pummelling from Hearts; most likely the reaction would have been to shout: 'Give it up – you're never going to win the Scottish Cup.' But the records show that twelve months after the Auld Reekie Deathmatch Hibs were back at Hampden. They also confirm, somewhat surprisingly, that Pat Fenlon was still the manager.

Hibs' route to the 2013 final wasn't straightforward. They beat Hearts to gain some revenge, though that thrashing won't easily be forgotten and any decent atonement would have to involve them winning the cup and doing it in style. They also had to defeat two other Premier League teams, Aberdeen and Kilmarnock, the latter overcome with a hat-trick from Leigh Griffiths, who was in his second season on loan from Wolverhampton Wanderers. Declaring yourself to be a Hibs fan, as Griffiths had done, is no guarantee the hard-to-please Easter Road constituency are going to swoon. A penny banger in a dustbin, he'd been booked three times for starting arguments with fans reluctant to show the team unconditional, uncritical love. But progress to another final, and Griffiths' own fine form, had gradually improved relations.

The cup wouldn't be won that year, though. Griffiths picked up an injury before the final against Celtic and was a doubt right up to kick-off. He didn't seem fully fit during the game, the first final to be played on a Sunday. But in any case he was never going to win the trophy on his own and this was a meek performance from Hibs who seemed content simply to have got back to Hampden, and to limit the opposition to three goals.

Neil Lennon's Celts were strong. They'd already won the Premier League and this was the season they beat Barcelona, the greatest club side the world has ever seen. This Champions League victory was destined for heritage-group status, to be reminisced about monthly. Celtic had Fraser Forster, Kris Commons, Joe Ledley and Gary Hooper, all a cut above what Hibs could muster. But they were beatable: St Mirren had proved that by dumping them out of the League Cup when John McGinn was an eighteen-year-old Buddy.

Celtic's star performer was Anthony Stokes. Often mean and moody, he was menacing that day, swinging in crosses from the left that made knees quake in the Hibee defence and led to Celtic's first two goals. No one thought then that Stokes and McGinn, both Hampden winners that year, would make Easter Road the next stop in their careers with the Celtic man having been there and done that. All we knew was what Hibs, despite casting off most of the men who failed so dismally in 2012 and finding places for promising kids like Alex Harris and Jordon Forster, had lost yet another final. This one finished 3-0.

These Hibs didn't seem to believe they could win – and two months later would be thrashed 7-0 at home by Malmo in the Europa League. Against Celtic in that final they were hunched and almost haunted in their demeanour, fearing the worst. By that stage even tabloid newspapers were using the unredtoppy word 'malaise' in connection with the club, such was the widespread belief that 'being Hibernian' was a medical condition, an extremely queasy one with no known cure. Regarding the Scottish Cup, if Hibs' ship was ever going to come in, it would almost certainly be HMS *Gardyloo*, the sludge vessel which chugged up and down the Forth and was named after the old Edinburgh tenement cry from a more dangerous age in sanitation, warning the lieges that a bucket of shite was heading their way at top speed.

There was, though, a key game in that cup run. In the semi-final against Falkirk, then a division below, Hibs produced thirty minutes of stunning slovenliness and when the third Bairns goal hit the net this was the crack of doom for some fans who hurled their scarves at the pitch as the most incompetent players were being substituted and then stormed out of Hampden.

A Glasgow cabbie told me how word spread across the taxi computer that there was good business to be had in the vicinity of the stadium: 'I picked up three Hibs fans in a terrible hurry, all with terrible faces on them. "Queen Street Station and quick," they said. I thought I should ask: "Everything all right, lads?" I wondered if maybe something awful had happened, an accident back in Edinburgh, family involved. "The team's crap," they said, "and here's how crap. We've already paid for a bus to take us back but we cannae wait until the end. We'll pay for this taxi and we'll pay for a train because we've got to get far away from Hibs *right bloody now*."'

I could have been among the bolters. Turning to my son Archie, then aged six and bearing a wee pinched look, I asked if he wanted to go. I wanted to go and it seemed like child cruelty to keep him there. No way, he said. 'Oh ye of little faith, Dad.' Actually what he said was: 'Do you see those orange trainers that boy's wearing – where do you think he got them?'

It amounted to the same thing, more or less. This was only his second-ever game. He didn't know that Hampden used to be majestic, he didn't know that Hibs had had the odd majestic moment in their 138-year existence and frankly he didn't care. He was starting out on the journey of being a fan and he wanted to experience all that it offered, the laughter and the tears.

Why is that man eating a pie when he's already had a pizza? Why does that man not like [infuriating full-back] Tim Clancy? If no one ever runs on that track round the pitch, why's it there? Are Hibs the worst team in the whole wide world? What did I think his sisters were doing right now? How many people did I think were at the game – seven million? Could I ask that boy where he got his orange trainers? And, most urgently, all the fans who've thrown their scarves away, will they get them back at the end?

So we stayed. And Hibs, incredibly, stayed in the cup. Manager Pat Fenlon confessed afterwards he thought about joining the first-half rush for the exits. Kevin Thomson, effectively playing for free in his second spell at Hibs, ripped into those drawing a wage for such a putrid performance. They came back out after the interval and scored four with a screamer of a winner from Griffiths.

When you're this young and this new and this alive to every possibility you soak up the atmosphere of a game you confidently predict will be the greatest you will ever witness just like a discarded scarf soaks up spilled pie grease. I didn't want to tell Archie that, in my experience, as a Hibs fan, it may well not get much better than this, a semi-final win from an unpromising position.

But I did want to thank my son for supporting me, supporting Hibs. If it hadn't been for him, I would definitely have walked out on my team and then, being too embarrassed that they'd turned the game around, stayed away from the final. And maybe that would have been it, finito.

My father used to encourage me in the difficult business of supporting Hibs, keep me believing when all hope seemed gone, catching me when I fell, and now I'm relying on a child for this.

Ridiculous, I know. The great popular verseman Roger McGough has a lovely poem called 'Bearhugs' about watching his sons grow up, grow taller than him. At the start of the piece, whenever the boys greet their father he says they're 'squeezing the life out of me'. By the end he's come to depend on their vigour, innocence and optimism and reckons they're squeezing the life in.

At hapless, hopeless and very nearly Hibs-less Hampden that day, Archie squeezed the football into me.

TWENTY-FIVE

'NO RANGERS, NO ANTHONY PERKINS IN A DRESS. PROPERLY DEPRIVED.'

MARVIN BARTLEY, THE toughest guy in the Hibs team, was like the disruptive boy in nursery ruining the structured play of the other kids – but in a good way. He marauded across the middle of the park in the semi-final looking for promising Dundee United moves to smash up.

Looking at him go about his work you might wonder if in his downtime he's a cage-fighting fan who likes his telly compiled from CCTV footage of lager-louts scrapping round the maypole of sundry English towns. But the day after the victory he's watching *Antiques Roadshow*.

The rest of the Hibs team and all the fans, all the football supporters in the world if you believe the breathless, screeching coverage, are tuned in to the other semi. It's Rangers v Celtic. The self-styled greatest derby of them all. The explosive fixture featuring the legendary foes who hate each other the most. A match with a clamour about it which is itself antique, referencing 300-year-old battles, and one that half the country would cheerfully not have to endure as it seeks to promote a modern, inclusive, go-ahead and, well, ever so slightly antiseptic Scotland. Others would claim it's not just Scottish football's USP but its OFR (only flamin' relevance). Ninety minutes of absolute pandemonium, loved by zealots and broadcasters, hated by polis and wives. In this particular case it lasts 120 minutes with

Rangers eventually winning on penalties and they'll meet Hibs in the final.

What kind of rivalry do Hibs and Rangers have? Immediate post-Second World War it was intense, the lustiest contest in our game, enacted before stupendous crowds – and entirely wrapped up in the seven First Division titles they split between them. Lawrie Reilly of the Famous Five told me there was mutual respect between the teams, if not a little apprehension in the Rangers ranks. 'They paid us the compliment of soaking the leather ball when we went over to Ibrox. It was like a horseracing handicap for us,' he said. 'One time I headed the big mealie puddin' and could remember nothing else about the match. But I was good friends with Rangers fellows like Ian McMillan and Willie Thornton and we'd stay with each other after matches and go to the pictures together. I even remember having toothache and Willie chumming me to the dentist. We were the two best sides in Scotland at the time and there was talk of our attack and their Iron Curtain defence combining for the national team. Sadly it never quite happened.'

*

For a middle-class boy living in Edinburgh's New Town, Rangers represented a rite of passage, and an elusive one. I was allowed bubblegum. I was allowed guns (toy ones). I got to wear my hair a little longer, though not quite to the Beatle moptop proportions I desired. The short breeks-only edict was relaxed when snow blocked the doorways. I got to upgrade my football boots from Winfield – Woolworths' own with their thick plasticky red stripe – to Adidas when the laughter wouldn't stop. But I was deemed not yet old enough for a game featuring John Greig, the two Willies, Henderson and Johnston, and the thundering Ibrox hordes.

The ban was down to the sheer size of the crowd, at least that's what my father said. It seemed to last for an incredibly long time, which of course made these matches all the more tantalising, and in my frustration I strongly suspected I had the most sheltered childhood in the whole of Scotland. This was absolutely confirmed the day *Psycho* became the playground rave. 'Did you see that barrie fillum last night?' I of course hadn't. The other boys could have been lying when they boasted of having been present when Rangers visited Edinburgh but there seemed to be too much detail in their critiques of Alfred Hitchcock for them to be faking having seen the daddy, or daddy-dressed-as-mummy, of horror flicks. 'And the knife went right through the shower-curtain and the blood was runnin' doon the plughole.' So there was me. No Rangers, no Anthony Perkins in a dress. Properly deprived.

Inevitably, when I was eventually allowed to attend Rangers games they weren't quite as exotic or scary as they'd been in my fevered imagination, although Ibrox captain Greig certainly possessed the most formidable arse. But there was an edge to the matches, you could sense it on the terraces, and this was quickly ramped up as the 1960s turned into the 1970s. Hooliganism came to football and the Troubles began in Northern Ireland. In The Shed at Easter Road, Hibs fans flew the Tricolour and sang 'Off to Dublin in the Green'. They might have been celebrating their club's Irish roots but they were also winding up the Rangers supporters. The contingent from Govan would retort with 'UDA all the way/Fuck the Pope and the IRA' but, really, games against Hibs were junior, starter-kit demonstrations of their Protestantism and deep love for the Queen and the union. The big test for them would be the Old Firm derby.

There was the odd sweet moment such as Christmas Day, 1971, a party at Easter Road when Rangers fans brought the bevvy. On what will almost certainly be the last-ever full card of fixtures played in Scotland on 25 December I still can't believe my father and I managed to sneak out of the house, leaving the rest of the family to the BBC panto with *Blue Peter*'s Lesley Judd as Cinderella and Tony Blackburn as Buttons, or that 25,143 others did likewise.

Easter Road was like one of those refuges for men – and it was all men that day – who have nowhere to go at Christmas or can't cope with the emotional stress. But in the spirit of peace and goodwill the cans of beer lugged onto the terraces – twenty-four per slab – were for once passed round rather than thrown. 'Get that doon ye, son,' urged a Rangers bear with the Red Hand of Ulster on his tammy, lapels and fist and I sipped my first Double Diamond which was both horrible and beautiful. The Gers were battered for eighty-nine minutes and then won the game at the death.

(*Rangers, Rangers, the pantomime villains of Scottish football, the Lee Van Cleefs, and we're playing them in the final . . .*)

My first visit to Ibrox – the Big Hoose – had been the previous season. More than an initiation, Ibrox for a boy, not yet man, is maybe best summed up by a line from the Beatles' 'Being for the Benefit of Mr Kite': 'Lastly through a hogshead of real fire!' Everyone should do it once. And if you think Ibrox is a challenging afternoon these days, corralled into a corner of the ground and required to peer between the Greigy-dimensioned constabulary backsides to see the game while being sprinkled with loyalburger crumbs from the top deck, then you should have been present at my initiation ceremony.

Pre-segregation, it was extremely easy to wander into the middle of what seemed like a secret society: old men in bunnets communing with younger men with wild hair and giant sheepskin collars, passing round the half bottle of Whyte & Mackay and passing on the traditions – not just of a football team but a way of life. This was where my father and I ended up that day, possibly through being unable to avert our gaze from stairway thirteen, hideously buckled from the Ibrox Disaster of a few weeks before, and not paying attention.

The anthems were declamatory. I remember thinking it would have been funny if the little light blue invalid cars circling the pitch had joined in the recital by parping their horns, but this never happened. Surrounded by dissenting viewpoints, in truth, didn't bother Dad. He liked a good argument although the provocative line I imagined he often took during those dinner-parties for grown-ups over the lemon meringue pie would not have gone down well in Govan. I on the other hand, for the first and only time in my life, was hoping Hibs were not about to do something stupid and win the game. Thankfully Ibrox's flat-fronted goalposts came to Rangers' aid, although there was still some local disgruntlement that the Hibees had snatched a draw. This was when I was briefly in danger of losing my ridiculously long green-and-white scarf. I think I impressed Dad by holding onto it, and he quickly calmed the situation, thankfully without calling anyone a philistine or a nihilist.

(*Rangers, Rangers, the stomping ogres, the team we love to hate, intent on keeping the hoodoo going.*)

Before those two games in '71 I just assumed that when Hibs played Rangers they had to take their medicine. Rangers would win – usually in the league and always in the cup. That Christmas, it would be stretching things to say we saw a great light. But as Dad and I walked home, glancing through living-room windows at pretty festive vignettes of snoozing and squabbling in front of roaring TVs, we started to think the Ibrox giants might be beatable.

*

This happened right away, which increased the aggro both on and off the pitch. Hibs under Eddie Turnbull were intent on smashing the great Old Firm carve-up. Rangers, still seeing the Hibees as ponces from the east, didn't like the idea of that one little bit. Okay, so some of the victories came in the Drybrough Cup but don't try telling Hibs fans that this short, curtain-raising tournament with minimal offside played on lush, warm grass with the boot-boys dispensing with Crombies to flaunt their braces was an irrelevance.

John Blackley and the two Alexes, Cropley and Edwards, were cultured footballers with an eye for a silky pass. They didn't hand in notes asking to be excused matches against Rangers, though; they got stuck in like everyone else and loved the jousts which raged through power strikes, games sometimes being shifted to afternoons to save on the floodlights.

Cropley, the slightest of players, even contrived a block-tackle which broke the toe of immovable object Greig. He remembers an X-rated challenge by Willie Johnston on team-mate John Brownlie, the same Ranger punching Jim Blair and being sent off and Alex MacDonald being 'quite a clever inside-forward at St Johnstone who went to Rangers and turned into a keelie who'd kick you from behind. Mind you, so did Alex Edwards'.

Edwards doesn't deny this: 'One time Tommy McLean had been annoying me all game so at the end I ran after him down the tunnel at Easter Road and just at the slippy bit I smacked him.' During another bone-juddering encounter with the Ibrox team he walked over MacDonald as he lay on the ground, leaving stud-marks on the player's chest.

Cropley says that even before Turnbull came along Hibs-Rangers games were combustible affairs, and especially in the Scottish Cup. 'The semi-final between the teams in 1971 finished nil-nil but we should have won. Our manager Dave Ewing called Rangers "rubbish", which was splashed all over the back pages. The replay had even more needle than usual.'

Amid the mayhem of these encounters, Turnbull, nicknamed Ned, still expected his creatives to show flair. Cropley again: 'Ned used to say to us: "Get out on that bloody park and express yourselves."' When Hibs beat Rangers in the replayed 1972 cup semi-final, Blackley remembers Rangers manager Willie Waddell coming into their dressing-room to congratulate the Hibees. 'After he'd gone Ned said: "You should have thrashed them. Only scoring two has kept that man in a job."'

Ibrox, the first time, was unforgettable for Cropley and this was the occasion of my knicker-wetting stumble through the flaming hogshead: 'I remember, in the away dressing-room, being struck by how high the pegs were. Was that deliberate to make us feel small? The Rangers team, in those light blue shirts with that big badge on it, always seemed huge anyway.

'When you came out of the dressing-room you walked past the training area where the police would be briefed for no doubt another busy afternoon. And I'll never forget what I saw down there: a big cardboard cut-out of the Pope with his arms outstretched. There were marks where balls had hit, so presumably His Holiness was used for shooting practice.'

Blackley was sent off at Ibrox, for disputing the kind of decision which visitors to the red-brick citadel believe has regularly been awarded against them since Rangers came into existence. 'Tommy McLean was miles offside when he scored,' says Blackley. 'Pat Stanton asked the linesman, "Which lodge are you in?", and I took it from there with nonstop swearing – I went absolutely mental. [Referee] Bob Valentine sent me packing and the SFA produced this charge-sheet listing every f-word and b-word. I was too ashamed to show it to my mum.'

Hibs' mastering of Rangers didn't last and by the time the Ibrox club were winning nine league titles in a row Hibs were being put firmly in their place with a 7-0 thrashing. This was just three short of the Hibees' biggest-ever defeat, inflicted by – who else? – Rangers on Christmas Eve, 1898.

Rangers lead the Scottish Cup head-to-head – fourteen wins to Hibs' ten and their victories include the 1948 semi-final watched by 143,570, a record crowd for both clubs. At the start of this century there was a flurry of cup-ties, the clubs squaring up every two years with Hibs only managing one win in the four-game sequence. After that a rivalry which was epic in the 1950s and ferocious in the 1970s lost its lustre. No one got excited by the games, no one got angry, and Hibs v Rangers became a routine fixture in a Scottish scene full of blandness and the underwhelmingly over-familiar.

*

Then suddenly it became *the* fixture. Rangers' financial meltdown brought administration, liquidation and the humiliation of being squashed into a cannon and blasted towards Peterhead, to begin life again in the pie-base tier of Scottish football. On their climb back up through the divisions they bumped into Hibs on the way down.

Hibs were shell-shocked and feeling sorry for themselves, blaming an ex-Ranger, Terry Butcher, for getting them into such a mess. Rangers were still hurting from their fall from grace and still resentful of every club who'd banished them. They wanted a scrap, Celtic weren't around, but Hibs with their new ex-Celt manager would do nicely.

In their first season together in the Championship, both desperate to escape, Rangers and Hibs met seven times with each game being more tempestuous than the last. They represented a big nostalgia trip if you could recall the duels of the 1970s, albeit there were no toilet-rolls flying across the sky, or what the booze-banning Criminal Justice (Scotland) Act on the back of match tickets would term 'carriers'. But these tussles were mere warm-ups for 2015-16 and the biggest crowds, the most provocative mind-games, the niggliest wind-ups and the snarliest hype.

On the opening day Rangers came to Easter Road in the Petrofac Training Cup, a booby prize for teams outwith the top tier with an unlovely name. It wasn't important – something Hibs were keen to re-emphasise after being whipped 6-2. This was the time of Rangers trying to prise Scott Allan from Hibs, the midfielder starting on the bench and being cheered by the Rangers fans when he appeared. Hibs could use the unsettling of their star man as an excuse but Rangers, in Mark Warburton's first game in charge, were impressively bright.

The first league game a few weeks later was preceded by Stubbs claiming that managing a club of Rangers' stature was 'easy' and Warburton telling him 'with respect, to shut his mouth'. Allan had gone but Hibs made sure Rangers didn't get him. That ramped up the tension, and meant that 49,220 weekend psychologists and part-time lip-readers were poised with anticipation for the pre-match greeting between the managers. Rangers won a tight affair by a single goal.

These central characters in the drama made for a sharp touchline contrast. While Stubbs was unflappable, Warburton was jittery and, in the kind of blue suit he probably wore in his previous life in the City, resembled an expectant father nervously pacing outside the maternity hospital having rushed across from the office.

Rangers then went on a long unbeaten run with the Ibrox faithful turning up for games with bread produced by the baker bearing the same name as their leader and singing a song about him having a magic hat. But Hibs ended that sequence, much to Warburton's astonishment. 'Very respectfully, there was only one team in it,' he said. 'How we've not won the game – again respectfully – I really don't know.'

By the time of the next meeting Hibs had caught Rangers, the two teams level on points at the top of the Championship. Such was the fuss and bother for this game back at Ibrox at Christmas that one veteran observer reckoned that the great festival itself had been overshadowed.

'We've got the best team and the best manager,' declared Rangers captain Lee Wallace. No, Hibs are not getting under our skin, insisted team-mate Kenny Miller. Oh yes we are, said Hibs. Stubbs claimed

Rangers were 'in denial' over his team's threat, impishly pointing out: 'Warbs can't even mention us by name!' Warbs, asked if he was feeling the pressure, said: 'Pressure is making sure you've got your wife a nice Christmas present. That's my only worry right now.'

Was he was enjoying the mind-games? 'It's more Amateur Psychology (Level 1),' he sighed. Ignoring the unwritten rule where managers don't talk about the opposition, Stubbs painted a picture of Rangers players' living-rooms when news came through that an injury-time winner had enabled Hibs to gobble up the last chunk of their rivals' lead and the chorus of cursing which greeted it.

Rangers won the festive fixture in front of what would be Scotland's biggest league crowd of the season – 49,995 – and would go on to be crowned champions before Hibs made it two league victories apiece, three days after we discovered the clubs would contest the cup final. Unless you were Marvin Bartley, of course, when you would have been in thrall to Fiona Bruce and her jackpot-denying junk-assessors.

(Rangers, Rangers, heading back to the big time, totalitarian rule, world domination – who can possibly stop them?)

So the engrossing drama is to have one more act. It should not be forgotten that Rangers and Hibs players down the years have had good respect for each other.

Apart from Lawrie Reilly receiving sympathy for his toothache from old Ibrox foes, Alex Edwards subsequently played golf and shared a drink with those Ibrox men he slapped and trampled across insisting: 'They weren't bad lads at all.' And Stubbs points out that during his battles with cancer he received hundreds of good-luck messages from Rangers supporters. 'They're decent fans,' he insists.

But a rivalry is what it is. If you cowered behind a terracing wall when finally granted parental permission to glimpse Rangers in the flesh – heaving chests, sturdy hurdies and oh those backsides – then you won't ever forget this. This is a club which, despite the recent problems, continued to reside in the Big Hoose while fans carried on drinking post-match in a pub styling itself as 'quintessential'. It follows, then, that their tumbles will always be mighty ones.

The match programmes I collect are kept in three boxes: Hibs games, Christmas Day games (in tribute to all the other fans who dodged Crimbo for the football) and one labelled 'Notable Rangers Defeats'. This important archive chronicles the Scottish Cup shockeroonees caused by Berwick Rangers and Hamilton Accies, Arbroath stunning Ibrox, Chesterfield triumphing in the Anglo-Scottish Cup, Jim Baxter inspiring Raith Rovers to victory in Govan and quickly being signed by Rangers, Alex Ferguson scoring a hat-trick for St Johnstone and later ending up there himself.

The light-blue legions won't be surprised at this. They have a song about how no one likes them, but everyone hates them. But the box amounts to weird respect.

TWENTY-SIX

'THERE WAS CEREAL AND TOAST AVAILABLE FROM 9.15 P.M. . . . '

LEADING THINKERS, TOP theorists, pre-eminent academics – in reality, more and more mischievous Jambos – are advancing the cause of 'Hibsing it'. But if the Hibees want to keep the term out of the dictionary, then late on in games they're going to have to keep the ball out of the net.

Between the semi-final and final of the Scottish Cup there is still an opportunity for another injury-time disaster. Indeed Hibs are leading Falkirk in both legs of the league playoff semi only to be mugged at the death twice. As sure as the grande dame in a crummy soap-opera will finish a phone call learning something to her disadvantage with a withering stare into the middle-distance, so the Bairns, with the clock showing red, will launch a long throw into the box. It's the way things are and, seemingly, always will be. Hibbies are beyond despair.

At Easter Road, Conrad Logan falls on the ball with enough force to burst it but somehow it squirms from under him and over the line and the tie is back to all-square. Alan Stubbs had restored Mark Oxley after the cup semi but the latter made a mistake in the league victory over Rangers. What does Stubbs do – revert back to Oxley again? These are the decisions which can make, or break, a campaign – and a manager.

'Mark wasn't happy about being left out, he didn't take it well,' says Stubbs. 'I left him for a few days and we had a chat. There was no ranting. Goalkeeper is the most vulnerable position.'

In the away leg Hibs are in control, seemingly headed for a showdown with Kilmarnock for a Premiership place, until: the grand dame scowls, the ball flies into the box, utter predictability ensues. There is huge misfortune over a penalty not given to Hibs and a red card not awarded against Falkirk but ultimately this is failure.

'It was a cruel way to lose,' says Stubbs, 'and what made matters worse was it was Falkirk.' The tetchiness between Stubbs and Falkirk's Peter Houston has been almost on a par with his spats with Mark Warburton of Rangers. After the last league game between the sides when Falkirk snatched a late draw with a goal from yet another long throw, Houston celebrated with a Gangnam-style dance – inadvisable manoeuvres for a fifty-eight-year-old bald man in a shellsuit. Houston also couldn't resist a jibe at the perceived mental fragility around Easter Road as the Championship reached squeaky-bum time when he promised that his side wouldn't 'Hibs it'. Stubbs says his players didn't deserve such a savage denouement to the league campaign. 'But football doesn't take any prisoners. Against Falkirk it pulled down our pants and whapped us across the backside.'

Before this clash, Hibbies were pondering the $64,000 question: cup or promotion? Stubbs, down near his apartment in Portobello, would be stopped by fans and told: 'My head says promotion but my heart says cup.'

'To me that was just . . . crazy,' he says. 'Getting back to the top flight had to be No 1. But at the same time I understood. I knew the cup had become this great, big, engulfing presence in the supporters' lives, or non-presence. I think the history, the turmoil, the abuse and the misery of not having won it for so long was becoming unbearable.'

No pressure then, Stubbsy. 'Well, you have to believe me when I say I never ever felt any. Maybe that was because the players gave me that confidence because their spirit throughout the season had been unyielding. It had been sensational. I never looked upon taking Hibs into the cup final as pressure. I saw it as an excitement and a privilege.'

The players were given two days off after promotion hopes died amid the wastelands of Westfield and returned to training on the Monday of cup final week. 'They came in sharp and bright; they all wanted to be back on the grass,' says Stubbs. 'Our preparations went well. We discussed Rangers strengths and weaknesses, how we had to stop their full-backs and not give their midfield a chance to get on the ball. I shouldn't say too much about their weaknesses – it wouldn't be fair.'

On the Friday the Hibees packed the bus for the journey to their cup final hotel, bypassing Mar Hall in Renfrewshire where they'd stayed for the League Cup final which ended in defeat and checking in at Cameron House on Loch Lomond which had been the base for the Scottish Cup semi. 'I'm not superstitious but some of the players are, so we went back to where we'd been for the Dundee United game. We got there early so the players could enjoy the spa facilities. Dinner was early and we had cereal and toast available from 9.15pm. I didn't want them waking up in the middle of the night feeling peckish.'

There was also food for thought in Stubbs' eve-of-final address. 'I spoke to them about cup final days and about how they could be the best days of their sporting lives,' he says. 'I spoke to them about becoming legends and about freeing themselves from history and of creating some of their own.

'It was a rallying call and it got quite emotional. I'm normally pretty composed but now and again it's no bad thing for players to see passion because we'll all human and that Friday night was one of those times.

'I told them to seize the moment because they might not get another opportunity, so they weren't to have any regrets. They had to walk out onto the park taking it all with them – from that first bit of encouragement with a ball from a father or whoever – everything including the kitchen sink. And they had to walk off the pitch not able to expend even one more bead of sweat.

'Then we spoke about what the day would mean to the fans, how the team bus on the way to Hampden would pass families with kids in the back of cars who would be in absolute awe of our players and that they should recognise that they had the power and not to be daunted by it – the power to make dreams come true and be remembered for ever.'

Something to ponder over the Rice Krispies, then.

TWENTY-SEVEN

TIME FOR HEROES

21 May 2016
Rangers 2 Hibernian 3

'A stranger can stay if he loves someone here, loves them enough to want to give up everythin' for that one person. Which is how it should be. 'Cause after all, lad, if ye love someone deeply, anythin' is possible.'

We're all vaguely familiar with Brigadoon, right? Even if you don't know that's a line from the film, even if you've never seen the movie, you'll be aware of the basic plot about a Scottish village which only comes alive every hundred years and then just for one day.

Sounds pretty hardcore. And quite apart from the irritation of your plumber not turning up on that blessed day, or the tragedy of only spotting the beautiful girl with the bouncing hair, gamboling in the distance, just minutes before century-long darkness descends, you would then struggle to get to sleep knowing that Scots everywhere would either be laughing at such a kitsch, kilted, kliched portrayal, or cursing you for setting back the nation's cause.

But if living in Brigadoon must be tough, spare a thought for the inhabitants of Hibsaredoomed. These poor, wretched souls can only hope to be relevant once every 114 years. Though if they don't win the Scottish Cup today, that'll become 115.

I love Hibernian deeply. Does *anythin' being possible* including beating Rangers?

Sometimes I think I might have loved Hibs, especially in the cup, just a little too much. In 1973, at the school youth club, I could have got off with Alison Donald. She was getting off with someone that night for sure and I was the main contender for some mooning – slow-dancing – to the Moody Blues' 'Nights in White Satin' but duty called me to Easter Road for the fourth-round replay against those self-same Gers.

The following year, when I should have been swotting for my Higher French, I was bunking off at the fifth-round replay at Dundee. Then in 1990 I sold my ticket for Murrayfield's Grand Slam rugby decider to head back to Tayside because surely after disposing of Dundee United this was going to be Hibs' year in the cup? Foregoing a great Scotland triumph, a respectable exam pass and a fumble behind the tuck-shop in a cheese & onion crisps/Charlie perfume miasma, I witnessed Hibs lose and lose and lose.

In darker moments I will try and convince myself that it was a Hibs cup-tie which caused me to miss a Hawkwind gig when the magnificent Stacia was still dancing topless to their whooshing space-rock. And a *Play for Today* about a liberated Swedish au pair causing havoc among a repressed British dinner-party set. I don't know if these clashes actually happened but I kind of want them to have done. And this is why Hibs' monumental failure to lift the trophy has got to stop. It's getting out of hand.

Being Hibs fans without the cup makes us feel odd for sure but also different and special. In darker moments – all moments, basically – this is what we tell ourselves. Now, football supporters can strain for some pretty perverse logic and this is a stunning example. What are we really saying: that winning the cup is somehow tacky and common? We're beginning to enjoy our own tragedy and given any more encouragement we'll be glorying in it. After 114 years we've reached peak hoodoo. We *need* to win the Scottish Cup. *Today.*

*

It's a beautiful day – big cowboy sky, warm sun, no wind. Everything is quiet and still and expectant. Well, apart from the tiny zephyrs of dread.

Hibs can beat Rangers but can they do it in a final? I have never seen this happen; indeed, it has never happened before. If Hibs regularly 'Hibs it' then Rangers have been fairly proficient at 'Rangersing it': that is, being the big team from the Big Hoose, sitting on heads, squashing pipsqueak challenges, confirming one of the hoary old certainties of Scottish football. Rangers usually win the Scottish Cup. They've done it thirty-three times.

'We may say that the western eleven throughout were too much disposed to give 'the dunt'.'

That's a line from the *Edinburgh Evening News* match report of Hibs' first, and only other, cup triumph against Dumbarton in 1887 but the description could easily apply to Rangers and especially the side of the late 1960s and early 1970s. Five years in succession they were drawn against Hibs in the cup, dunting them out in all but one of the ties.

The stout men of Ibrox were too strong in 1969 and 1970 while in the semi-final the following year, a 'shambles' of a match according to *The Scotsman*'s John Rafferty, the referee 'pandered to the destructive players'. No football, no goals; Rafferty hoped for better from the replay but was required to report that 'the attacking of the [Hibs] forwards was as the flapping of dove wings against granite rock and cup-ties can't be won like that'. There was more flapping from Hibs in 1972's semi: the team didn't believe in themselves and allowed Rangers to 'push them around like they were second-class citizens', according to one report. Then at last the Hibees produced a brilliant cup performance against Rangers, winning at the second attempt.

In today's papers few seem to be predicting any more brilliance from Hibs in what will be Alan Stubbs' 100th game in charge. Indeed with Rangers having clinched the Championship some weeks before and heading back to the big time, the man from the *Daily Mail* forecasts a 4-0 romp for them.

The Govan garrison have always been extremely well-drilled. Forty years ago this happened on the dunes of Gullane, East Lothian under the ferocious command of ex-jungle fighter Jock Wallace, and Alex Miller, a former Ranger who went on to manage Hibs, once provided me with a vivid description of the torture: 'We changed into our kit in the beach car-park in full view of the day-trippers while Jock rammed poles into the sand. He kept hold of one of them and Derek Johnstone would get a whack: "Lift yer fuckin' knees up!" A young lad, George Walker, collapsed. He got given oxygen but then it was: "On yer fuckin' feet!"' In the afternoon the players were afforded a break from running across the dunes. Instead they had to yomp up Murder Hill – sixteen times.

Mark Warburton strongly disapproved of Wallace's methods as an apprentice under him at Leicester City. No way to treat footballers, he said. But his Rangers appear just as steely than the old brigade and, worryingly, they play with more flair. They've had a nice break since wrapping up the league while Hibs have been slogging their guts out in the playoffs, ultimately in vain.

Gulp.

*

I'm going to the game with my brother Sean and oldest Hibee chum Rab who're gulping even harder and faster than me; we've all been thoroughly battered by recent events. Thank goodness, then, for Archie who's been up since six, practising John McGinn three-sixty turns since one minute past and is currently selecting his cup final attire from an Elton John-dimensioned wardrobe of replica polyester. His great-grandmother used to call him 'such a solemn boy'. If only she could see him now: he can't stop smiling and his eyes are sparkling like champion marbles.

Archie, the Atomic Rooster, wants us to belt through to Hampden right away. No need, son, I say – it's nine hours until kick-off. I tell him we're fortunate: we can have breakfast, kiss Mum and the girls goodbye and travel in comfort, and while the Euroblobby people-carrier parked outside lacks the sexiness of my father's Lotus or the stateliness of the Riley, it will deliver us safely and on time. Some fans, back in 1887, had a more challenging journey to the national stadium:

> 'Several Edinburgh working men, at present unemployed, took to the road on Thursday night for the purpose of seeing the match at all hazards, while a number of miners, currently on strike in the Airdrie district, also walked to Hampden for a similar purpose' – Evening News.

A North British Railways football train left Edinburgh with 1,000 supporters and the large Irish population living on Glasgow's outskirts had their own specials. There was a break-in at Hampden and the paper wondered if the walkers were among the 3,000 to gain free entry. 'The excitements caused by the prospects of the final tie could not be overstated,' its report said. Neither can the excitements caused by this one. Or the angst or the doubt or the prissy faffing. My last domestic duty of the morning is to help get my daughters changed into their ballet costumes but I cannot perform even this simple task without inducing floods of tears (theirs, not yet mine). We're waved off by my wife with a cheery scowl which I translate to mean: 'If you're not going to win the thing after all those years don't bother coming back.'

The classic route. I bang on about this as if it's the road to Bethlehem when all you do is come off the M8 at Junction 15, turn right at

Glasgow Cathedral while admiring the redoubtable Adam-designed Royal Infirmary, travel down the old High Street imagining teeming life when this was the city's medieval heart. For what are Hibs fans if not, however reluctantly, students of history?

No doubt there are quicker ways to get to Hampden than via the Gorbals where, on my first trips, squat, embattled pubs hung on grimly while all around had been condemned and flattened. No doubt there are places to park nearer the stadium than Brownlie Street but this is where we stop because of time-honoured tradition, even though it has never brought much luck. It has to be Brownlie Street because of John Brownlie, the Turnbull's Tornadoes right-back, and no man so winged-ankle-dashing has ever been saddled with a nickname like Onion.

Lunch on Hampden days used to be tricky – the solitary Chinese restaurant my father and I could find was always jam-packed – but not any more because there's an Asda with a cafe and plenty of grassy knolls around the great bowl for alfresco dining. This store sells everything. 'Which item would you have most difficulty getting through the turnstiles?' asks Rab. 'The BillyOh Kentucky charcoal grill barbecue retailing at £79,' suggests Sean.

Pre-match entertainment is another vague concept at Mount Florida, at least since the demise of Middle of the Road and King the Alsatian. There's a fine football museum under the main stand but it's never open on matchdays. I guess it would have difficulty coping with 50,000 admissions all at once, which is a pity, as that's the kind of audience the great artefacts deserve, none being greater that the sheepskin jacket worn by Archie Macpherson while delivering *Sportscene* commentaries from his gale-battered scaffolding eyrie. The museum also displays behind a glass case a designer gutty, just the one, left behind by a Hibs casual after a spot of organised hooliganism. Is this my club's claim to Hampden fame? Something altogether more edifying is urgently required.

We find a spot to eat our sushi – as I say, we are Hibs fans – and a busker plugs his guitar into an amp. Because our club are semi-regular visitors here, just not anytime winners, this troubadour has gone to the trouble of learning most of the Hibs songbook. It's strange hearing the tunes sung in a Glaswegian accent and in these versions the Hibees are 'famous' rather than 'mental'. We're shouting out requests – Sean for the one about 'Super' Joe McBride, Rab for the paean to Jimmy O'Rourke and how everyone knows his name – when suddenly there's a huge roar. It's the team bus. The players wave, the fans wave back.

The players look relaxed, the fans look petrified.

One record goes today. For seventy-eight years East Fife have proudly called themselves the only Scottish Cup-winners from the second tier there have ever been. We count up the number of people who've confessed to a 'funny feeling' that the Hibees are finally about to do it and have been keen to impart this info to us. Does the whole country, other than Rangers and Hearts fans, want us to win? There's a thought, and there's more pressure. Pat Fenlon, the last manager to get the club to the final, used to complain that 'Hibs blow it again' was the story everyone wanted. He was convinced the world was laughing at us.

Not wishing to appear ungrateful but 'funny feelings' doesn't seem terribly scientific. We're talking about Scottish football's great tragedians. About a grotesque narrative which has tormented five generations of Hibbies. We are – are we not? – the biggest chokers the country has known since Jane Franchi was forever concealing her lovebites on the telly quiz *Superscot*. Surely we're going to need more than a hunch and a fond hope, but we can't procrastinate any longer. It's time.

'Time for heroes' reads a Hibs banner across the far side of sold-out Hampden. Rangers hoist one of their own: 'We'll meet again, don't know where, don't know when.' It's a jibe about them leaving us behind in the Championship but in referencing Vera Lynn this almost qualifies as the sweetest message ever to pass from Govan to Leith. It's sheer bedlam in the national stadium. 'Hibees, Hibees' is the chant from one end, 'Rule Britannia' booms out of other. One set are 'huns', at least until First Minister Nicola Sturgeon bans the word, while the other are 'spoon-burners', inferring they're all on heroin. Unlike that Christmas Day game between the teams, no one is going to be passing round the Double Diamond. Hampden may not be the colosseum it once was but the start of a Scottish Cup final is still an assault on the senses, a paintstripper aperitif before the boisterous vaudeville for the masses properly begins.

What's even better than this final at three o'clock is the match at the 3.02 p.m. mark. Hibs have scored. It's the goal Anthony Stokes has been trying to fashion since he arrived: a jittery run up the left wing, ball on a piece of string, then some more Chaplinesque paddling to disguise the quick, smooth, killing finish. Wheeling away in celebration, Stokes disappears into the red, white and blue firecracker fug at the Rangers end. Will he ever re-emerge? Did we just imagine that?

This doesn't feel real. The final is playing out in a fantastical, dream-like manner. It's the final, the performance, that other teams muster, not Hibs.

'McGinn in the centre put in powerful work' – Evening News

That was Peter McGinn in the 1887 triumph but John of that ilk is crashing into tackles, winning ones he shouldn't, and so are David Gray, Liam Fontaine, Fraser Fyvie. This gives the contest a retro feel, and the referee is definitely officiating in a 1970s throwback manner and letting the game ride. Rangers are shell-shocked. Their fans try to lift the team with their version of 'Wand'rin' Star', a 70s hit for a growly Lee Marvin. All we need are the stadium roofs to unhook and float away, Pat Stanton and Alex MacDonald to come down from old-warrior hospitality and Archie Macpherson to grab his sheepskin from the museum and we'll be right back there. It's free-form like football used to be, with Hibs doing most of the period reconstruction and letting rip with a stats-busting number of attempts on goal, almost all of them from Stokes.

Conrad Logan: I roomed with Stokesy the night before the final and in the morning he was awake before me, looking keen, and I just had this feeling: he's up for this. He's a great lad but some days it didn't look like he was doing a lot. That day every time I got the ball I just tried to zing it out to him. He was unplayable.

Alan Stubbs: It was the day when we saw the real Anthony Stokes. He terrorised Rangers down their right the whole game. They didn't know what to do, whether to go tight or drop off. With Anthony in that kind of mood I wished we could have played Rangers every week and so did he. He was sensational.

Hibs being Hibs, though, we should expect the storyline to oscillate wildly. For half an hour Rangers do next to nothing and then in the thirty-first minute James Tavernier flings over a cross, the imperishable Kenny Miller sneaking the equaliser. Now it's Hibs' turn to be stunned, all apart from Stokes who views Rangers' riposte as a personal insult. This was going to be his final, what's the big idea? He paddles murderously and biffs a shot from twenty-five yards which almost breaks a post in two. Miller winds up the Hibs man some more with a header which rattles the bar. Stokes throws himself at a cross just before half-time, narrowly failing to get his luxurious rug on it. It's been a great final so far, at least if you're a neutral.

If you're a Hibby you might think you've seen this movie before. The team blaze into the lead which, given their gruesome heritage in the tournament, is ridiculous, incredible and almost makes you wonder: are Rangers, mighty Rangers, going to let us win? Rangers start that sluggishly, Hibs begin that urgently. Then Hibs are reeled in with the minimum of fuss which, on the basis of the gruesome heritage, is entirely predictable.

Still, the fans are trying to stay optimistic. The chant, as the players head down the tunnel, is once again 'Hibees, Hibees'. In the Turnbull's Tornadoes era my father, who once famously declared that Hibs would win the cup eventually, alerted me to how this clarion-call would be issued at a change of ends at Easter Road, and especially if the team were then heading down the slope. I certainly remember the shout at halftime in the 1972 League Cup final, after which a good performance turned into a great one.

But it's Rangers who score next. Hibs pick up where they left off with the two outstanding features of the first half – Gray's tigerish tackling and Stokes' desire to get his shots away as early as possible, almost as if the ball is stolen property and he's stashing it from the just-arrived polis – receiving further embellishment. The team seem to be in a good position, or rather as good as Hibs can ever be, and fool that I am the memory-box marked Notable (Though Obviously Not Scottish Cup-Winning) Hampden Goals gets opened and Stanton, Brownlie, Alan Gordon, Ally MacLeod, Stephen Fletcher and Leigh Griffiths are being glimpsed again through half-shut eyes. I can remember where on the pitch the strikes emanated and it's a careless indulgence. For suddenly I'm recalling where Rudi Skacel was standing for the fifth in the 2012 final because just after the hour-mark Andy Halliday fires a rocket from roughly the same position.

We're right behind the strike and so can follow its deadly zing. It's a tremendous goal, a goal fit to win the cup and potentially the kind to shatter a team's belief, convincing them that even though they've strived, passed brightly, been bold and brave, been the better side, this simply isn't going to be their year. *Again*. This is no consolation but the glorious failure of 1979 is under threat: 2016 is shaping up to be the best performance in a losing final in the club's history.

Jambo jokes and jibes are being readied. The Hibs fans can almost hear the gurgle and churn of social media. Were the team to lose, further humiliation would come three days later, for at some point during the afternoon of 24 May it would then be a million hours since they last won the cup. I look over at my brother, my good friend and my son. To be honest, Archie appears the least likely to burst into tears. He is young, unswervingly loyal, ever-hopeful – and only really knows great Hampden comebacks. But he isn't the only one in the stadium staying positive.

Conrad Logan: The manner of the Halliday goal was annoying because we switched off a bit in the middle of the park but I wouldn't say I was that bothered by it because I looked at the clock and there was plenty time left. Maybe being raw to the club that was the optimism I had. Perhaps some of the lads were thinking of the Hibsing it thing: they'd been leading in the cup final and now they were losing. But to be honest I didn't see much evidence of despondency among them. They'd been the better team, there were flames coming off them! Right from the restart they went all out to retrieve the situation.

Paul Hanlon: Because I'd played for Hibs in two finals and lost I might have wondered: 'Have I missed my chance?' But I honestly always thought that I was going to be part of the team that lifted the cup. I know: it might have been difficult to make that stand up in court! Where was the evidence? But the lads kept believing. There was a sense of injustice among us. We'd battered teams in games and got no reward. We were playing some great football against Rangers but we knew that if we lost we couldn't trot out yet another hard-luck story. We weren't prepared to lose that game, simple as that.

Alan Stubbs: I had to change from a back-three to a diamond because we were behind in the game. In the midfield Fraser and Dylan [McGeouch] had been doubts beforehand and I had to ask them to be honest and tell me whether they were 100 per cent fit because they had to be to play in the final – they couldn't be selfish about that. Their answers were truthful so Liam [Henderson] started on the bench. He took that brilliantly and that's another reason, beyond his ability, why he's got a great future ahead of him. There are others who wouldn't have taken that decision quite so well.

Liam Henderson: Keats [James Keatings] was asked to warm up and I thought to myself: 'I'm not getting on today.' Then Rangers scored and I was told to get ready . . .

From having played an intense match up until that point, Hibs then start to perform as if their lives depend on the outcome, which in a sense, trying not to be too melodramatic, is true. After 114 years they deserve a break. The good, gloomy people of Hibsaredoomed deserve to see the sun again. Hibernian FC deserve the Scottish Cup. But it won't just fall off an MDF plinth into their laps.

For all the progressiveness and invention today, we know this team can play, and that under Stubbs they tend not to muff their lines in the big games. The really striking thing about this performance is what in 1887 was known as 'the dig'. What in the 1970s would have been the desired response to a cry from the terraces of 'Gerrintothum', not that the Hibees of that era were leading exponents.

Like Atlético Madrid with knobs on. That might describe Hibs' tackling. Or how about Atlético carrying hammers? McGinn dives into a stramashful situation and has no real right to emerge the gasping potholer, still in possession of the ball. Then in the eightieth minute Darren McGregor, somehow finding himself in the old inside-right position, wins a challenge that is no more than 30-70 in his favour. Fyvie barrels forward and wins a corner. Henderson pierces the Rangers defence at the near post and with a flick of Stokes' head the final is all-square.

Alan Stubbs: I missed the goal – toilet break! As I was leaving the changing-room I heard a roar, but didn't know which team had scored because the TV pictures were a bit behind the action. Rangers were on the ball and maybe I thought they were about to head upfield to put the game beyond us but Darren came away with the ball, I don't know how. That epitomised the desire and belief of our players and every single one of them showed it. Who was prepared to make that tackle, run that extra ten yards? We had the guys who were willing to do all that and more. When you have that desire and belief then anything is possible and on the day they achieved the so-called impossible.

'Hurry up, Hibs!' was the cry in 1887, inscribed on cards to be worn in hats and given to fans when they piled off the Hampden-bound trains. But what is happening here? We've entered the period in previous games where it's all gone horribly wrong for this team but this time they're sending the script for a re-write. The green-and-white half of the stadium is quivering with anticipation and not, as is traditional, in a bad way. Anxiously, I turn to my son. 'Are you okay, Archie?' I ask. He says: 'You've asked me that six times already, Dad, and please stop holding my hand so tight.'

What is happening? Random players, games, goals, incidents, facts and life-or-death ephemera tumble across my mind like rubbish being blown across an empty terrace . . .

My first game, 19 August, 1967 vs Clyde . . . My first goal, a Joe Davis penalty . . . The pong of pipe tobacco from the city's pale ale moguls and toffee tycoons lighting up after a profitable week . . . My first night game, also my first European game, Leeds United winning via the goalie's four-step rule – sensation! . . . The Vitoria

Guimaraes keeper throwing flowers into the crowd, me catching the bouquet, spoiling my junior boot-boy look, not modelled with much conviction in the first place, the Clockwork Satsuma . . . the portrait of my father with the Hibs match programme in the pocket of his purple safari suit (very *Rowan & Martin* party-scene, Dad) . . . the club phone-number in the programme, ABB 2159 . . . George Best arriving at Hibs and tripling the crowd, Pat Stanton leaving and halving it . . . Eric Stevenson, then at Ayr United, bunking off to watch Hibs win the League Cup and being fined . . . the Harry Gilzean cartoon-strip of that triumph as brilliant product-placement in the *Trainspotting* movie when Renton, the spoon-burner, goes cold-turkey . . . the Hands off Hibs banners in Genoa at Italia 90 . . . the Hibs supporter in Naples playing keepy-uppy with oranges for beer money . . . Johnny Graham, Johnny Hamilton, Johnny Aitkenhead . . . the accelerator pedal jamming on the classic route to Hampden . . . an Alsatian stopping the search for a parking place on another Glasgow excursion by thumping its front paws onto the bonnet . . . the 'Get them out in the semi-finals' cry of an old *Edinburgh Evening News* deputy sports editor who didn't fancy the extra work involved in further progress . . . my father's back-of-a-ciggy-card biog of himself: 'An inveterate, incorrigible, ineluctable Hibernian fan' . . . the last game I watched with Dad, a League Cup final, Rangers winning in injury-time . . . my childhood prayers by the side of the bed: 'Please God, keep the family safe, make Nicola Coombes have an accident in Chemistry so I can save her and she'll get off with me, and please, please, please God, make Hibs win on Saturday . . .'

They're desperately trying to win this Saturday. It's like this will be the last football match played anywhere, ever. Hibs are in such a hurry that even the manager has come to the touchline to ensure speedy retrieval of the ball. Gray hurls himself into a challenge, Lewis Stevenson does likewise on the other wing, then the pair of them tackle each other, Stevenson coming off worst and needing treatment. Gray charges into attack, the move breaks down, he charges back and gets hurt. Stubbs will laugh as he tells me that 'David likes a bit of drama, he enjoys the suspense of us not knowing if he'll be able to continue'. Well, he's at the right club for drama and suspense.

Niklas Gunnarsson warms up and it seems that the captain's final is over but, no, Gray hobbles back into the action and must be impressed when the lofty Norwegian makes a timely interception. The play is so frantic and yet now it seems to be happening in slow motion. I consider fainting – a pretend-collapse like the one aged fifteen at a Roxy Music concert prompted by the saxophonist, Andy Mackay, flipping his instrument upside down to parp a thrilling refrain – but pull myself together and burst into tears instead.

The ninety minutes are up, stoppage-time: Gray stalks Nicky Clark from behind, hassles and bothers him, and the Rangers man appears to kick the ball out of play in a bid to stop all the aggravation. From the quick throw Fyvie motors across the park, and sets up Stokes who flashes a shot from a tight angle which is saved.

Henderson gets ready to take his second corner . . .

TWENTY-EIGHT

'I RAN INTO TAFF'S BIG JACKET IN FLOODS OF TEARS AND HE KEPT ME IN THERE FOR A GOOD TWO MINUTES'

LIAM HENDERSON THINKS it's now up to five or six. The number of Hibs fans who've had the words of Sky Sports commentator Ian Crocker turned into a tattoo. And that's just the ones who've tweeted him photos. After the final Henderson went on holiday to Ibiza with Jason Cummings where the pair hooked up with John McGinn. Bumping into the three young blades was too much excitement for a supporter who told them he was rushing off to the nearest tattooist to have the legend inked on his sunburned ankle. No need to do that on my part, said Hendo, but the fellow returned later to show off his inscription:

'Liam Henderson to deliverrrr! . . .'

So, come on then: while Gordon Smith, Willie Ormond and others were undoubtedly responsible for some sweetly-struck despatches from the flags – and Patrick Callaghan fired over the ball which led to the cup-winning goal in 1902 – what's the secret of the *two* most important corner-kicks in Hibee history?

'I've always fancied myself at dead-balls – I like hitting them,' says Henderson when we meet in a city centre coffee shop. 'Every Friday at training the gaffer would say to me: "Hendo, go and hit the corners." So I'd done that for a full year and against Rangers we knew what we were going to do.

'The main thing was that [James] Tavernier was weak at defending corners – he cannot head the ball – so that's where the first one was going. I've always done something my grandfather read about [English rugby kicking legend] Jonny Wilkinson: how he used to focus on a speck in the crowd, maybe a red hat, and aim for it. In our final there was the top of a letter on a banner just above Tavernier's head so that was where the corner was going.'

(Now you're probably thinking of Homeland or a similar US boxset drama where portly general-types sit round an over-polished table in semi-darkness and watch modern warfare play out on a fuzzy black-and-white screen. As often happens, a key target is fixed in the sights and chillingly turned to dust).

'I looked at my point of focus for about four seconds,' he continues, 'chipped the ball into my hands and placed it so I'd strike the valve – that helps me get it up and down. Then I flicked my hair behind my ears. The game was frantic at that stage and I have to relax myself to take a good corner and that's the way I do it. It always annoyed [John] McGinn. 'You and your hair,' he'd say.

'Myself I love reading about dead-ball technique. How did [Andrea] Pirlo do it? That kind of thing. I'm back at Celtic now so I've been asking Scott Sinclair from his time at Chelsea how [Didier] Drogba did it. But a good corner needs a good header and Stokesy produced a great header.

'For our winning goal I knew I wasn't going to hit Stokesy again. Surely Rangers had wised up. So – exactly the same routine although, sorry, I can't remember what in the crowd I was aiming at – I decided to send the ball two or three yards further back. There's a stat that eighty per cent of goals from out-swinging corners hit the net at the far post. I managed to get the whip I needed and obviously Dave [David Gray] has shown the desire and the rest is history.'

You have to remind yourself when you meet Henderson that he only turned twenty a few weeks before the final. You have to remind yourself he was a loan player at Hibs, a role others seem to view as downtime or somewhat beneath them. This is a hugely impressive young man, thoughtful and grateful. Grateful for the chance to play football, for the sacrifices, support and mentoring of others, and to Hibs for giving him 'absolutely the best year of my life and one day which, if twenty-four hours was all I was allowed on this earth, I would happily take'.

As you can tell, he speaks well. 'It's weird, this relationship between Hibs and me,' he says. The loanee has returned to his parent club but still hankers after what he had at Easter Road. 'It's like I've split up with my girlfriend but am still in love with her.'

Henderson, not getting much game time at Celtic, was desperate to come to Leith previously and disappointed a loan couldn't be worked out. When the idea was revived, he was 'intrigued and excited' about the prospect of working with Alan Stubbs, plus there was a strong Hibee tradition in the family. Three generations including dad Nick, who played for Partick Thistle and Hamilton Accies among others, supported the club.

Already knowing Jason Cummings from Scotland Under 21s, he quickly hit it off with the rest of the team. 'It was some dressing-room,' he says. 'It was a place full of laughs and full of jokes and I went into training every day with a smile on my face. Myself, Jason and John [McGinn] had a joke about how in years to come when the three of us were fighting it out for the Ballon d'Or people would say: "And to think these guys all played for Hibs at the same time!"

'I loved being around Paul [Hanlon], Stevo [Lewis Stevenson] and Daz [Darren McGregor] who're such big Hibs supporters and who wanted this cup so much. And I was also fortunate to have Thommo [Kevin Thomson] as my mentor. The oldest roomed with the youngest and we got on great.'

Henderson was an instant hit with the fans who loved his passion and what seemed like unalloyed joy at simply being selected for the team. 'I've had a bit of stick about the way I celebrate goals. Scoring for Celtic against Partick when I was seventeen I went off my head. I don't know what it is, maybe the feeling that my next goal might be my last. I'm very fortunate being able to play football for a living and at Hibs I wanted to show it means something to be out there on the pitch. Fans want their team to win and I'm the same. I've hated losing since I was five. Back then I used to cry.'

Henderson didn't start in the fourth round at Raith Rovers but appeared in the second half and, he feels, made a difference. 'The next day at our recovery sessions Raith mentioned on Twitter that the last two teams who'd put them out of the cup had gone on to win the trophy so we were all joking: "It's in the bag."'

One of the wonderful mysteries of the cup run is how Henderson managed to eke out the cross for Cummings to spark the comeback against Hearts. 'Jason and I have always kidded on that we're telepathic and don't even need to speak on the pitch. We just clicked right away. I put that ball up to him without looking and it was some header he made.'

A key staging-post on the journey, he says, was the away dressing-room at Tynecastle when the team revved up the Proclaimers on the docking-station, albeit that 'Sunshine of Leith' ended abruptly. 'Did Hearts cut the electricity? That's what someone said.' After the replay victory Henderson was convinced Hibs would go on and lift the cup, though he never told anyone about his premonition.

He was devastated by defeat in the League Cup final. 'Not for myself because I thought I might be lucky enough to get to play in more finals but for the older guys like Dave, Daz and Fonz [Liam Fontaine]. I was crying my eyes out for them. I couldn't stop thinking that I'd let them down for two whole weeks.'

Back in the Scottish Cup he might ordinarily have been left out of the replay at Inverness, as often happened in 'the more physical games', but injuries to others meant he had to start. 'I thought I needed to show the gaffer I could do the dirty side of the game as well. It's something I lack so I tried to wind up their guys and kicked a few of the bigger ones. But I knew Big Marv [Marvin Bartley] and McGinn would have my back.'

When the penalty was awarded in the semi-final Henderson was convinced Cummings would attempt a Panenka. 'But I wasn't annoyed at him because I knew how many games Jason had won us.' Defeat in the league playoffs was a shattering blow but Henderson rode it out. 'The way I look at life, some things just aren't meant to happen and for some bizarre reason we weren't supposed to beat Falkirk although obviously we should have done. I'm quite good at coping when bad stuff happens. There was a plan in place for us and I took it to mean the Scottish Cup. And here's the thing: I don't think we'd have won it if we'd managed to get promoted.'

Henderson knew he wasn't going to start the final when four weeks before he'd been left out of the final league game against Rangers as Stubbs stuck to his preferred back-three to combat the Ibrox side. 'I was disappointed but I spoke to my dad who told me to stay positive and be a good teammate. I think I was that because earlier in the season when I wasn't picked a couple of times I went in the huff.

'The final was nerve-wracking to watch although Stokesy scoring so early was brilliant. I think he's an incredible footballer. At 1-0 maybe I wasn't going to get a chance but warming up at half-time when it was all-square I was thinking: "I'm going to come on, I'm going to change the game." Hopefully that doesn't sound big-headed but I always think I can influence matches, be it against Rangers, Alloa or Barcelona.'

Influence it he did, and after the first brilliant corner followed by the second diamond-studded delivery, there was still time for another Hendo cameo, much cherished and revisited. 'There was a free-kick right at the end should have been awarded to Rangers, 100 per cent. But something I learned from an Under 14s final: when you know there might be a question-mark over a decision, be decisive. That's why I purposefully grabbed the ball and rolled it along the grass back to big Conrad [Logan]. Some folk don't reckon I'm a thinker!'

So what about the last remaining seconds when he seemed to position himself as close as possible to the referee to receive first intimation of full-time with the blast of the whistle before beginning his mad gallop across the park – was that deliberate?

'To be honest, those seconds are a beautiful blur. I was running in the direction of my mum and dad because without them I wouldn't have had the chance to play in a final. Hibs had won the cup and I was crying. I'm not scared to admit that I was in floods of tears and couldn't stop. I ran to Taff [coach Andy Holden]. He was wearing his big jacket and he kept me in there for a good few minutes.'

Henderson thinks the post-final party lasted six days although it might have been even longer. 'I remember Fonz saying: "That's us meeting up pretty much every year around this time for ever now." It's a bond for life and that's a great, great thing.

'I think about the final a lot. It's brilliant to watch back if you're sad about something and even better if you're happy. I've returned to Celtic because I want to try and made a go of it with them but I love Hibs and want the fans to know that and how much I love them. Would I want to play for them again one day? You bet – a hundred per cent.'

TWENTY-NINE

'THERE'S SOME PEOPLE ON THE PITCH . . .'

JUST WHEN IT seems that the lads have ran out of footballs for the Leith Walk version of the Eton Wall Game, a tenement window opens and another plastic sphere is donated to the celebrations.

The object of the game is simple: blooter the ball as high as you can. There are cheers when it lands on a bus shelter, loud roars when it bounces off the roof of a No 16 – and cries of 'You must be a Jambo!' when it clears the tall spire of Pilrig St Paul's Church and disappears.

'This is surreal,' says Angus MacKay, one-time Labour MSP and full-time Hibby, drinking beer outside Robbie's, which is bursting at the seams and spilling onto the Champs d'Leithie like every other pub on this night of nights. 'From the start of the game – did we really score right away? – until right now it's been like a big, strange, sexy dream. Directed by some mad French dude – Luis Bunuel, perhaps. I really hope the sensation is permanent, that it's going to last the rest of my life.'

After putting my son to bed – cuddling his match programme, tooter, flag, giant foam hand and green-and-white scarf bearing the legend '21 May, 2016' – I've headed down to EH6 and it's hard to disagree with MacKay's assessment. Watching Hibs in the Scottish Cup used to be like having your eyeballs slit with a razor, as happened to a young woman at the start of Bunuel's *Un Chien Andalou*; not any more. In the happy chaos – footballs flying, cars honking their horns, group hugs of ten or more – I bump into a succession of friends and fellow travellers, each more happy/teary/disbelieving than the last. Round the corner from Robbie's, the Tourmalet is possibly more of a Fellini-esque pub. Every face is characterful, like they're all members of a travelling circus. Is anyone working the bar or do we just serve ourselves? No matter: everyone looks beautiful tonight. Grown men, old men and tired and emotional men sing the Alan Stubbs song. Then they sing the John McGinn song. Then: 'Your defence is terrified/Coz Stokesy's on fire.' My phone buzzes with congratulatory text-messages – two ex-girlfriends and one Hearts fan, the latter being Jim, retired policeman and old school friend, who summons more names from our Hibee-Jambo playground banter by asking: 'Was that you on the pitch with "Snatch" Trotter and Kenny McPike?'

I wasn't on the pitch but Kieran, the humanist minister's son, was. 'I got a bit for you,' he says, handing me a clump. It's my turn to attempt a straightforward three-pint transaction which might take forever. At the bar I inspect my turf trophy which is immediately trumped by a fellow I've met before. This is Andy who, wouldn't you know, was on the pitch when the Tartan Army sacked Wembley in 1977. His wodge – the Hampden one – is in his tobacco pouch. 'I'm going outside to smoke it,' he says. 'I got a bit of the goal-net, too, and if I ever get home I'll smoke that in front of the telly, watching the final all over again.'

'When the whistle announced the suspension of the game, hundreds of spectators rushed to the pavilion and accorded the Hibs a great reception' – Edinburgh Evening News

That was 1887 and the first cup win. In 2016 there were some people on the pitch. They *knew* it was all over. Hibs had won the Scottish Cup. At last. So they ran down the Hampden steps like they'd been freed from some dreadful incarceration such as a hijacked plane and streamed onto the park. Many of them looked like they had no idea how they got there. They were having an experience which was both out-of-body and out-of-hoodoo. They cavorted, hugged, posed for selfies, ran about, stood in quiet contemplation, stretched their arms heavenwards in gratitude, sunk to their knees and kissed the grass.

Some tore up bits of what had been the Rangers penalty-box and sat on the crossbar under which David Gray had bulleted his header. A smaller number ventured up the other end, celebrated in front of the Rangers fans who came down onto the pitch for a full and frank exchange of views, with Ibrox players caught up in the mayhem.

Hibs winning the Scottish Cup was a great story for the match correspondents but the Hibees Hibsing their own victory party enabled some to continue with a favourite narrative. There was a long delay while the pitch was cleared and the team, who'd been cooped up in their dressing-room, were denied a lap of honour. Thus the final images of the day were unlike any in the competition's history: players lifting the cup in front of a torn-up park with its broken goal-frame while a line of snorting police horses made sure the slavering cup-crazed hordes, back in the stands again, stayed calm with unconfirmed reports that their Bovril had been laced with bromide.

There was hell to pay for a while. Police made arrests, sentences were handed down and the SFA set up an inquiry. In his findings – which didn't please Rangers – Sheriff Principal Edward Bowen QC said the vast majority of Hibs fans who ran onto the pitch did so 'in a spirit of jubilation'. The invasion, he concluded, had been the result of the 'exceptionally high degree of excitement'. M'learned friend could say that again.

*

Andy, the pitch-smoker, is fifty-five and has a highly respectable and worthy job which he would rather I don't mention but let's just say that he knows about the importance of valuable artefacts being kept both acid-free and lignan-free so the piece of Hampden that doesn't go into his roll-up will be preserved for evermore, just like his piece of Wembley.

'The two experiences were quite different,' he tells me when we meet for a coffee close to the start of the victory parade after tracking him down via a fansite. 'I was sixteen in '77 and into punk rock. I was patriotic then, not any more. I went through the motions of hating England but I'm married to an Englishwoman now. The day before the game a fan died jumping into a fountain and there were vigils for him. Maybe it was through naive eyes but that whole weekend seemed carnivalesque. When Johnny Rotten sang "Anarchy in the UK" some people thought he wanted to set up a Marxist commune and grow his own tatties but he said later that his idea of anarchic behaviour was the Scotland fans that day. I liked that.

'After we'd won my pals and I were swept onto the pitch. The vibe was good-natured and when some lights in the stadium were turned off – this was TV shutting down – the police removed their helmets, asked for some beers and played cards with the fans. A lot of turf had disappeared – it rolled up like carpet. A tarpaulin had been dragged to the centre-circle and it was moving. Even though I hadn't had sex by that stage I knew what was going on. The chick crawled out first, followed by the guy.

'I never saw any shagging at Hampden but I think quite a few folk were in the mood! There was incredible hysteria that day, understandably so. When the winning goal was scored everyone around me was holding the person next to them. It was like you'd fall off a cliff if you didn't. I've taken a few drugs in my time but I've never experienced a feeling like that. It was bottom-to-the-top. I was levitating.'

Andy, when he was younger, continued to make the biannual

pilgrimage to Wembley and much as he enjoyed bumping into the
hard-bevvying Rod Stewart and Elton John on these excursions –
though his musical preferences were for the Fall and the Slits – he got
fed up with the Tartan Army's loutish behaviour and so concentrated
his fan devotion on Hibs.

He has sound Hibee credentials. 'I grew up in Niddrie Mill, just
across the road from Pat Stanton's parents. Keith Wright lived down
the road and Leigh Griffiths was always firing balls into my mum's
garden. Aged five my dad took me to Leith Links for Gordon Smith
re-claiming his amateur status and there were grown men in the trees
craning to see him. I used to skive school to watch Hibs train at
Hunters Hall. Usually there would be fifteen of us competing to be
the best ball-boy, only the day Joe Baker returned there was a hundred.

'But a lot of the time Hibs were a tough watch. They were terrible
in the 1980s. I'd come to the conclusion my team just weren't going
to be allowed to win this cup and against Rangers this time I didn't
think they had a hope in hell.

'There's a conspiracy theory from Alex Miller's era as manager when
referees and linesmen before Scottish Cup ties apparently got given
gifts by the home team. Hibs lost a tie to a blatantly offside goal and
the linesman was asked later why he hadn't flagged. He's supposed to
have replied: 'Twelve cans of pish-for-lager gets you fuck all.'

'Against Rangers we've always been given nothing. Paco Luna
was sent off for the ball bouncing off his head and hitting his hand.
Mickey Weir was sent off for protesting about an Ally McCoist goal
after Andy Goram had swallowed his tongue. I used to come away
from Ibrox with my clothes covered in spit. After the 1979 cup final
the police directed our bus through a housing scheme where every
one of our windows was smashed and old men were running out
of their houses to throw more bricks. My friends are staunch but
philosophical. Irvine Welsh is a pal, he was on our bus, and when he
found out five guys didn't have tickets for the match he bought them

hospitality. But none of us fancied our chances of winning the cup.

'I didn't have a problem with fans running onto the pitch. That was joy, relief and a reaction to all the goading the fans have suffered for years. When I turn on the radio and it's Allan Preston [ex-Jambo pundit on BBC Scotland's Sportsound] I always feel he's goading me. Well, he can't anymore!'

'There was an older woman with an American accent sat behind me at Hampden – it was her first-ever football match – and at the end she said: "Bet you're happy now." I told her that a lot of the fans were orphans, taken to see Hibs by a generation of dads, mums, uncles, whatever who never got to see our great day, and that I was one of them. She said "I'm sure yours are looking down right now" and then I gave her a big cuddle.

'My parents did their – good word – winching at Easter Road watching the Famous Five. Dad was a champion piper but suffered pneumonia and pleurisy and died thirty years ago while Mum, who was just as big a Hibby, passed away last year. I wore Dad's scarf celebrating the 1964 Summer Cup win to the final and I was pleased to bump into an old pal, Martin, who was wearing his father's scarf – the classic dark green design with the thin white diagonal stripes, beautiful.

'When our bus got back to Edinburgh there were a few rainbows in the sky, including one which – you better believe it – ended at Easter Road. I'm sure that was Mum's doing, her request at the pearly gates: "I want Hibs to win the cup and I want rainbows."'

*

Another Hibby, Paul, is a marketing manager with RBS. In his office every day there is sober, circumspect and prudent decision-making. 'My first instinct, when my son Aidan asked if we could go on the pitch, was to say no,' he explains. 'But then I thought: "I've hugged everyone next to me in the stand – who else can I hug? Aha, all those other people on the park!"'

Paul, forty-eight, was at the game with assorted members of his family though not his wife Yvonne who was shocked when he phoned to say what he was doing. 'I reminded her she'd been on the pitch at Firhill with me when we won the First Division in 1999. Then she told me there had been a kerfuffle. From where we were, wandering around, enjoying the happy scene, taking photos, we couldn't see it.

'What happened was unfortunate but there was high-jinks which got out of hand and more significantly an outpouring of emotion which was unstoppable. It was a completely unexpected outcome: Hibs winning the Scottish Cup.

'When David Gray scored there was panic all around us. People were crying, shaking, praying, heads in their hands, unable to watch, muttering delirious gibberish. I thought to myself: "This'll be the mother of all Hibs failures if we don't win the cup from here." Then I thought of my father-in-law and Yvonne's uncle, big Hibbies who died over the past year.

'This was a millstone round our necks. We were the world record-holders at failed attempts to win a trophy. But not anymore.'

*

Lawrie, fifty-two, a lightning protection engineer, is indulging in his favourite hobby when I find him – mosaicing. 'There's a piece of my work hanging under the Famous Five Stand – it's of the Hibs crest,' he says. 'The one I'm making right now is of great lines from the end of the cup final commentary: "Hibs are standing on the brink of history" . . . "What kept you, Hibs?" . . . and everybody's favourite, "Liam Henderson to deliverrrrr".

'There were ten from the family at Hampden including my son Harry and his Swedish girlfriend. Beata is a prim and proper retired minister's daughter and that was only her second-ever game. At the final whistle, in that endearingly forthright Scandinavian way, she said: "I want to go on the pitch." I said it wasn't really allowed and Harry, who's as gentle as a kitten, wasn't of a mind but she was adamant: "We'll go onto the pitch. Isn't it what football fans do? And you must take a photo of me to send to my father."'

Like Paul, Lawrie didn't see the trouble. Like Andy he didn't himself procure turf but was given some later by a friend. 'I've planted it beside my dad's grave,' he says. 'Hibs are a community club and the old man was in the heart of it, running the Loch Inn at Lochend and also a builder's yard at Sunnyside. He was a huge fan who named me after Lawrie Reilly and took me to my first game in 1971, which for Hibbies was five unsuccessful Scottish Cup finals ago, but we don't have to talk about them quite so much now. The family had a wee ceremony at Liberton Ceremony. We thanked all the Hibs sides from the past and we thanked Alan Stubbs and his team for winning us the cup at last. It was lovely.'

'STOKESY NEVER GAVE ANYTHING AWAY AND YOU NEVER GOT CLOSE TO HIM. I DIDN'T MIND THAT.'

PAUL HANLON RECKONS he knows what won Hibs the Scottish Cup – Alan Stubbs' serenity. 'The manager was as cool, calm and collected with us as he was out on the touchline,' says the central defender. 'Even after a bad defeat he was never grumpy and always said 'Good morning' to everyone the next day. He didn't show the stress – and the season was extremely stressful – and that was great for us.

'He never panicked. If he had, that would have made us panic. The season we got relegated the manager [Terry Butcher] panicked and that spread to the players. 'Stubbs,' he adds, 'had a way of looking at things that was, I don't know, *real*. There was no falseness about him. He was always laidback, unflappable and assured. You trusted him and you thought: "I believe in this guy, I'm going with him." For me, that was how we won the cup.'

I meet Hanlon in a pub at Midlothian Ski Centre after a punishing training session led by demanding new manager Neil Lennon. As a Hibs fan who watched the club lose a cup final, then as a player in the worst final defeat the club could ever suffer, triumph after disaster was sweet indeed.

'I was struggling with injury towards the end,' he says. 'My knee was swelling up and my thigh was massive. I carried on until Stokesy equalised and watched the last ten minutes from the bench, which was agonising. Someone took a photo and everyone around me is so excited but me I just look ill. Then Dave scored the winner. No one deserved that more on the day, he never gave up on anything. The ice pack was off me and I got straight back on the pitch to be with the boys. Amazing.'

Hanlon says he can only really talk about the 2012 debacle of losing 5-1 to Hearts because Hibs have finally smashed their cup hoodoo. 'The Hearts final was awful, just awful. When they got to five there was still plenty of time for them to score more. I was just trying to do my job as best I could, although obviously it hadn't been going well up until that moment.

'Afterwards I was picked for the drugs test. Andy Webster was doing it for Hearts and he came into the medical room covered in maroon and white confetti. I couldn't look at him. That night I didn't want to turn on the TV because the game would have been all over it and the same with my phone. Where I was living at the time there were a few Jambos and more seemed to come out of the woodwork. I couldn't get to sleep for all their parties.

'I remember the night before that game I was rooming with Ian Murray and James McPake came to say that if Hibs won he wanted Ian, who was the club captain, to lift the trophy with him. That got me quite excited, maybe too much so, and probably burned up some energy.

'I usually room with Lewie [Lewis Stevenson] and I did this time. He's my best friend in football and we're both the same, pretty quiet. We've been through a lot with Hibs: all those horror-shows, the two cup finals when the team didn't turn up. But neither of us mentioned, say, the 5-1 game before this final; we just watched a bit of telly, had our supper and went to sleep. If I'd said something about how we had to wake up the next day and make folk forget all about what Hearts did to us Lewie would have said: "Well, obviously, mate." He would have wondered if I'd got the line from a corny movie or something!'

As a fan, Hanlon travelled to Hibs games on a bus organised by his father Derek which left from the Prison Officers' Social Club at Longstone, and he was a disappointed eleven-year-old when the Hibees lost the 2001 final to Celtic.

The bus still runs and this time ferried Derek, Hanlon's mum Sandra, sister Lisa, wife Danielle and all the lads who've seen him graduate to the team. 'My family have supported me every step of the way. Danielle's had to deal with me coming home raging after those horrible defeats. So it was great to have them all at Hampden. For me, winning the cup was like a big thank you to them.'

The way football functions now your club can have just as many loan signings for whom it's a temporary address as fans-turned-players. Alongside the trio of Hibee diehards this time were three guys who were just passing through but did so brilliantly, singing 'Sunshine on Leith' word-perfect as the cup was hoisted, and Hanlon pays tribute to them.

'What a great character Conrad [Logan] was. He might have been a wee bit out of shape but that didn't affect his agility. He wasn't fancy or flash, just a reassuring big presence – that's the kind of goalie I like. I'm sure the fans had a bit of a laugh when they saw him in the semi-final but he won us that match.

'Hendo [Liam Henderson] was brilliant. Some loan players turn up and it's like they're there to fulfill an obligation and you're left in no doubt it's temporary and after they leave you never hear from them again. Hendo wasn't like that and as a result was proper loved at Hibs. He was desperate for us to do well. He was desperate to get on the ball at every opportunity – you'd think he was a twenty-nine-year-old with 300 games behind him. And he was desperate to celebrate goals. We had a word with him – "Calm down, Hendo." But it made no difference, he went mad every time.'

And what of Anthony Stokes, hero and enigma? 'He did his own thing. He came in and did what he wanted. He never gave anything away and you never got close to him. But to be honest I didn't mind that. He's done some stupid things in the past – like all strikers, really. But he wasn't a bad egg who brought the dressing-room down.

'I suppose everyone thought he'd rip up the Championship and score a barrowload of goals but it had been months and months since he'd played and he was always going to be rusty. At times that was frustrating because you knew he could be great but he saved his best game for when it mattered most.'

When Hanlon scored the equaliser in the fifth round against Hearts he thought there was no better feeling to be had in football. He was wrong, and remembers the thunderous acclaim of the Hibs fans after the replay victory as hugely significant. 'The fans won it for us that night and their reaction at the end, belting out "Sunshine on Leith", made the newcomers in the team think: "This is a proper club."'

After the final whistle at Hampden, after DJ Dylan McGeouch's selection of bouncing tunes on the bus back to Leith, Hanlon made sure his parents brought his grandmother along to the party at Easter Road. 'My nana's my biggest fan. I never knew my grandfather – he died before I was born – but she used to tell me that every other Saturday he walked all the way from Broxburn to watch Hibs. Any mention of me in the papers she puts in her scrapbooks. When we played in the mint green strip a few years ago there was a big photo of me in the club shop. She asked the staff: "How much is that?" "We're not selling it," they said. "Well, let me know when you're taking it down." Now every time I visit her I'm greeted by this life-sized me, which is well weird.'

THIRTY-ONE

'SOMEONE TOLD ME IT WOULD BE BUSY'

'From many windows in St Mary's Street and the High Street lime lights were burned while other enthusiastic individuals greeted the conquerors by waving pieces of linen and cotton from a sheet downwards' – Edinburgh Evening News

That was the cup-winning parade of 1887, sweeping across to St Patrick's Church in Edinburgh's 'Little Ireland' where the club were formed. Maybe, because the 2016 team weren't allowed a lap of honour at Hampden, much is expected of the latest procession.

'At the end of the game no one could believe it: Hibs had won the cup,' says Conrad Logan. 'The lads were zapped. They were hugging, hanging off each other, the emotions were flying. They were a little bit out of it for a while. But when we were told we wouldn't be able to run round the pitch with the trophy we were like: "Really?" We were hacked off. Our fans weren't going to come back onto the park and the Rangers lot had all gone home. The attitude of the authorities seemed to be: "You've mucked it up for us, now we're going to muck it up for you."'

The parade starts from the City Chambers with a reception hosted by Edinburgh's civic leaders who, since Hibs' last victory, had reason to fetch out the best china for Hearts on no less than five occasions. The local authority's HQ sits above the Cowgate where the Hibs story began, where lime lights were burned to celebrate the first success – and where after 1902 prayers said in St Patrick's for another victory are supposed to have craved it any old way.

I never believed this. I didn't want a dire final, a jammy Hibs, a winner bouncing off a convenient backside, and I'm not sure many fans did. We wanted our club to win the cup the beautiful way, or the thrilling way. They went the long way about it – the 114-year way – but got there in the end.

Lead changing hands three times? The team losing with ten minutes left? Grabbing the winner right at the death? Just a blockbuster of a game? That's the scenario you daydream about in the dentist's waiting-room or somewhere equally inauspicious. It belongs in a comic strip with a vapor-trail whoosh for the hurtling ball.

Alan Stubbs, as ever, is calm as David Gray's header causes a lovely silvery ripple of the net. 'Obviously there's delirium going on around me,' he says. 'David gave everything in the game – as did the whole team – and he put everything into that goal.'

Logan says: 'As soon as he made contact with the ball I knew it was in. I like celebrating goals from the far end and at that moment I was down in my knees.'

*

From the High Street the open-top bus heads down North Bridge to Register House where the 1902 procession was 'completely circled by a moving mass'. It's pretty similar this time only the Duke of Wellington, captured in bronze on horseback, is wearing a Hibs scarf and so's his charger.

Before getting on the bus, Paul Hanlon was chatting to Dylan McGeouch who said that during his time at Celtic the Scottish Cup-winning celebrations would be 'ten guys, max, going out for a drink'. Victory parades can't happen in Glasgow for fear of upsetting the other half of the city and Celtic must also suffer from trophy fatigue. 'I told Dylan our procession would be massive,' says Hanlon. '"What do you mean?"' he said. "Mate, you've no idea how many fans are going to be there." "Brilliant," he said. But I was telling him that and even *I* had no idea how many fans were going to be there.'

'Someone told me it would be busy,' says Stubbs, 'but I never for one minute expected so many people to come out for us. The crowds just grew and grew. When we got to the Balmoral Hotel one of the guys said: "Turn around." I looked back and all I could see were people. They went all the way back to where we'd started and they were following the bus. Heading down the hill towards Leith there were definitely one or two more.'

The Duke of Wellington points in the direction of the port but there's no need. This bus knows where it's going. Among the rest of Edinburgh's statuary, Rabbie Burns and Sir Arthur Conan Doyle are also displaying Hibs favours and there are unconfirmed reports that Sir Walter Scott, quill-pen author of *The Heart of Midlothian*, is similarly adorned. Across from the Playhouse Theatre my daughters, normally only ever seen in pink, are dressed in green-and-white. A tourist from Argentina wanders out of his hotel and asks what all the fuss is about. 'Soccer?' Yes, I say. 'League?' No, cup. 'Which?' Hibernian. 'Ah, Scotch Cup! Long time. Long, long time. I know this. Congratulations my friend!'

If uptown is a riot then Leith Walk is sensational. The favourite thoroughfare of discerning Edinburghers and members of the People's Republic of Leith, it will sell you soor plooms, brilliantly-detailed models of Haymarket shunters, second-hand Atomic Rooster LPs, blow-up plastic dolls, blow-your-head-off snuff from Syria and boasts no less than three Swedish bars – it's a smorgasbord of quirky character and vibrant individuality. Today, though, everyone wants the same thing: to see the bus, the players in their crumpled cup final suits, and the trophy. The holy grail, the holey pail.

In the seventeenth century the Walk hosted executions of warlocks and witches. These must have attracted a few onlookers, as would the last man in Britain to be hanged for blasphemy, but not a turnout like this, swelling to 150,000 all the way down to Leith Links.

'I've been on parades in Leicester and very nice they were but, you know, fairly standard,' says Logan. 'The Hibs people were saying this one would be special-special and I was like: "Okay, we'll see." It started at ten deep, fairly standard, but then we turned a corner and there was an ocean of people. They were draped off lamp-posts, sat on bus shelters and cuddling the statues but it was the old folk up at the windows who got me: little, frail eighty or ninety-year-old grannies waving Hibs scarves. These people have waited a long, long time. I welled up when I saw them.'

There's a shop on the Walk called Borlands and it's an institution. Everyone knows what it sells even if they've never been inside. On one window the big sign reads 'Darts', on the other 'Television'. Truly, this is a day for splashing out on a set of its finest arrows – 'and since we've won the cup I'll take a telly as well.'

We will re-run the final constantly. The comeback from 2-1 down if there's time. From the equaliser to the end if we're in a hurry. Or the climax of swooping corner and rocketing header if we simply want a ten-second high to set us up for the day. We will find newspapers and receipts dated from before 21 May and we will smile while remembering our old lives and how much anxiety and yearning they contained. We will remark, when someone gets snagged up in life's little complications, and even fairly big ones, that it's okay, it doesn't matter, because we've won the cup.

Right away, a theory is propounded that being a Hibs fan has lost some of its romance because the Sisyphean struggle is over. Maybe the cup will corrupt us, like the innocent inhabitants of a remote island who finally get television. Maybe constantly re-watching of the victory on our Borlands tellys will turn us flabby and complacent.

'I can die happy now,' some will say while still young men which might sound over-dramatic but Hibs have been exactly that on their interminable crusade.

I don't have to search for Gordon Smith goals anymore (unless I really want to) and I don't have to wonder how the goals I saw Turnbull's Tornadoes score weren't enough to win the Hibees the cup (unless I really want to). The cup is right here. It's going along the bus from McGeouch to Fraser Fyvie to Liam Henderson to John McGinn, a tight-passing midfield to the end.

And it is the end for this team; they will never play together again.

Henderson, back at Celtic, will be anxious to deliver a last message: 'I've not had the chance to say thank you to the Hibs fans. I'm so grateful for everything they and the club did. I can't really put into words how special Hibs are to me.'

Logan at Rochdale will feel the same poignancy: 'I made a connection with Hibs; you don't always do that if you're a loan player. Before the final I got cards put through my letterbox down in Tranent. "For Hibs No 1 fan" was one of them, and "fan" had been crossed out. They all said: "Go and beat the Rangers". I'd have love to have stayed. The gaffer was going to sign me and then he left. That's football but it's kind of sad.'

Anthony Stokes – banging the side of the bus while singing the John McGinn song and catching bottles of beer chucked up to the top deck by fans – will go to Blackburn Rovers. He's been like the mysterious stranger in a corny B-movie who's wandered into a town in peril, saved it, and left again without saying a word – and after delivering one of the great cup final performances the faith of the man who phoned him for help has been justified.

Stubbs got most things right. From his early appreciation of the soul of the club to the tactics in his 100th game. He returned flair to the pitch and brought class to the dugout. At Rotherham United he will say: 'I think about the cup final quite a lot, to be honest. The hours and days afterwards were too hectic to properly appreciate what the club achieved.

'I've had a lot of letters sent down by Hibs fans. They tell me about their day and in some detail too. They mention who was with them at the final and in many cases who wasn't because the wait for the cup had been so long. Just last week a Hibs supporter even turned up at a Rotherham fans' forum.

'When we'd won it I thought of my dad and how much he would have enjoyed the occasion. I was pleased my own family were there to see their old man achieve something as a manager. I had a lump in my throat at the final whistle when John [Doolan, his No 2] came up and hugged me as he'd lost his father a few days before. I wanted to say something to him but it came out mumbled.

'But the special feelings I have about that day concern the players and the fans. The joy on the players' faces, seeing them get their reward for all their endeavour, was brilliant. And when I got the chance to hold the cup at the end and I was showing it round the stands, that was me saying to the fans: "This is yours." The players won the cup but when all's said and done in football the glory belongs to the supporters and, boy, did these Hibs fans deserve it.

'Fans are constants. The rest of us aren't, we move on. Hibs fans had to wait a helluva long time to feel that good. Even though I was only at Easter Road two years I could feel their pain. Hopefully the cup made up for all the disappointments, all the nearly days, all the bad days.'

I remember those days, and recalling them now, with the cup glinting in the Leith sunshine, they no longer seem quite so tragic. East Fife's Bayview with its rubbish floodlights isn't a black hole of third-round despair. The rain falling on Clydebank's Kilbowie isn't bone-rottingly wet. Arbroath booting us out of the cup isn't ridiculous. Humiliation at Stirling Albion? Part of life's rich tapestry. Now weebly-wobbly Dixie Deans has turned into Nureyev, making his hat-trick easier to thole. Now Arthur Duncan soaring for the tragic own goal in the *War and Peace* Final is proof, at last, that man can fly.

So Hearts hammered us 5-1. And your point is, caller?

The bus reaches the bottom of the Walk where the cheers, if anything, are louder and lustier. 'They were proper going for it down there,' says Hanlon. 'All the diehards were steaming and someone was giving a drum a good battering. That was when it felt like we were bringing the cup home.'

The fit o' the Walk has many regulars with favourite vantage-points for watching the world go by and among them is Queen Victoria. She's sporting a green-and-white scarf at a particularly jaunty angle and others who congregate here will swear by a new Leith legend that, on this day of days, her statue finally breaks into a big, beaming smile.

The Scottish Cup, home at last. It will take time for those of us down here, cavorting with an old monarch who died the year before the last victory, to process this information and accept it as fact. But my father, up in the High Stand with the other serene and all-knowing dads, was right: Hibs would win it one day.

ACKNOWLEDGEMENTS

THANKS TO NEVILLE Moir at Birlinn and Pete Burns at Arena for suggesting the book. Thanks to my editor at *The Scotsman*, Ian Stewart, and sports editor, Graham Bean, for putting up with the grand obsession for three months. Thanks to friends and colleagues who gave me valuable encouragement and advice including Rab McNeil, Alan Pattullo, Simon Pia and Donald Walker, also my brother Sean. Thanks to Kerry Black in *The Scotsman*'s library. Thanks to Richie Gillies for putting me in touch with Liam Henderson. Thanks to the players and fans who gave me their stories. Thanks most of all to my wife Lucy and our children Archie, Stella and Sadie for their love, support and – a key word, this – perseverance.

And thanks to Alan Stubbs and his players for winning the Scottish Cup.